REMEMBER

A Boyhood in Auschwitz, Dachau,
and with the Angel of Death

The Rittmans, father and son

DANNY RITTMAN

REMEMBER
A BOYHOOD IN AUSCHWITZ, DACHAU,
AND WITH THE ANGEL OF DEATH

iUniverse books may be ordered through booksellers or by contacting:

iUniverse
1663 Liberty Drive
Bloomington, IN 47403
www.iuniverse.com
1-800-Authors (1-800-288-4677)

ISBN: 978-1-5320-0018-8 (sc)
ISBN: 978-1-5320-0020-1 (hc)
ISBN: 978-1-5320-0019-5 (e)

Library of Congress Control Number: 2016911010

Print information available on the last page.

iUniverse rev. date: 08/04/2016

Life was good and easy, and I called life 'friend'. I'd never hidden anything from him, and he'd never hidden anything from me. Or so I thought. I knew everything. He was an awfully intelligent companion; we had the same tastes (apparently) and he was awfully fond of me. And all the time he was plotting up a mass murder.
– Wyndham Lewis

CONTENTS

ACKNOWLEDGEMENTS

THE AUTHORS WOULD LIKE TO thank family members for sharing photographs and recollections from early years, and Rebecca Rittman for the wonderful illustrations in this book. We also thank family friend, and the editor of this book, Brian Downing, for inspiring support and sound advice.

PREFACE

Sometimes I wonder. If we could remember everything from the moment of birth to the present, would we better understand how we arrived at where we are? We'd see small private moments and immense world events. Some things in our control, others far beyond it. This is my story – pieces of the past, from my entrance into the world to the end of the Second World War and the founding of Israel.

Hope ended suddenly as Europe began a descent, but persisted here and there. Fortune kept me from death many times and left me wondering about meaning and purpose in life. I do not know how or why I survived what we now call the Holocaust. Millions of others did not. Many of them were close to me, if only for a brief time – sometimes just before their deaths.

There were consequences. Neither religion nor spirituality resonated with anything inside me. Indeed I *despised* anything related to religion. Old age and longer shadows have softened me, but I cannot say my view has changed greatly.

Embarking on a new life in a new land, I found meaning in family and country. I served both. I devoted my life to Israel, a land that looked impossible in the past, only a dream, the topic of elders' dinner conversations. But it turned into reality. Better days arrived. Days of purpose. Days of beauty.

The darker period will always dwell in me. As I get on, it eddies up more and more. More than I like, and at unexpected times. I'm retired now and have plenty of time on my hands. The past takes advantage of the absence of daily routine, and it demands attention.

For those of us who experienced those dark days, all that is left is to wait. Wait for something we can never forget, and should never forget, to at last unburden us.

My son once read me a quote he'd come across. The words were said by a great spiritual leader, one of many whom I never believed in, but in whom I can see wisdom.

> *Light need not combat and overpower darkness in order to displace it – where light is, darkness is not. A thimbleful of light will therefore banish a roomful of darkness.*

Reading those words once, twice, and even three times made me see their beauty and power. They are indeed wise. They encapsulate what I've experienced and why I am here today.

My story is marked with occasional dark humor. It is an essential part of who I am which I acquired in late boyhood. It's been a close companion ever since. Paradoxically, dark humor can both illuminate and liberate, as I hope to show.

I'd like to accomplish something more here than answer family members' questions which I either avoided or responded to briefly, incompletely, and above all reluctantly. I hope to *inform* people, and I hope those people will *remember*.

HOME AND SEPARATION

T HE STORY OF MY FAMILY'S early days I learned in later years from my aunt, brothers, and sisters. The story is nonetheless part of my life, as much as your family's lives and settings are parts of yours.

My father Solomon was born in 1887 and my mother Hermina in 1900. My father owned restaurants and coffee shops in towns we lived in. Europe's economy was faring poorly in the thirties. Markets crashed, banks failed, shops closed. Our family moved from place to place trying to improve our prospects.

Two years before my birth, my family moved from a small town called Valea lui Mihai, which means "the town in the valley," where my father had a coffee shop in the train station, to Focsani – a medium-sized town with a population of about 100,000. It had factories, businesses, and vineyards in the surrounding countryside. My father worked most of the day in a small restaurant he opened, and my mother took care of the house the family rented on Bucuresti Street.

My parents had their first daughter, Viorica, in 1923, and one year later had my brother Maurizio, who was called Motzu. My father wanted to open a restaurant in Constanza so we moved there, again hoping to do better. In 1928, Rosy, my second sister, was born. I was born January 1, 1930. New Year's Day. A new start. Family members called me Shuly.

That same year my family redecorated the establishment and offered better food, but we still lived day to day. The Depression was beginning, and simply getting by was hard.

In 1935, a second brother, Lucian, was born while my family was living in Ploesti for a short time, where my father was trying another restaurant venture. My mother had another baby just before me, but he died during birth.

<hr />

It was an October night when my uncle Joseph Davidovich came to visit us in Focsani. He was my mother's brother and lived in a small town a few hundred kilometers away called Alba Julia. He visited every few months and sometimes we traveled to see him and his family. He was married to a beautiful woman named Catalina. Their son Yanosh was fifteen years older than I was.

Joseph Davidovich was a tall handsome man in his late thirties. Thin, with a small, neatly trimmed mustache, blue eyes with a penetrating look but always a trace of a gentle nature. He was better off than we were. He bought and sold miscellaneous goods in marketplaces and worked long hours. He owned a truck, which he used to travel to buy items from people and sell them to others for a small profit.

His large suitcases were full of merchandise of all types and styles. For a child of my age, they were exotic treasures. When he opened a suitcase, we kids would marvel at the watches, old coins from across Europe and the Levant, kitchenware, antiques, old toys, and other gizmos. I did not recognize many of the items but I knew they were not to be found in local stores very often, not until Uncle Joseph came to town.

He'd let me look through the cache and if a small toy caught my eye, he'd smile and present it to me. His travel and eye for value brought success. He owned a spacious house in Alba Julia with a large backyard. Uncle Joseph was a very special man and was significant for me during my childhood. As a matter of fact he was like a father to me.

"We eat stew only on weekends," Viorica said with practiced assertiveness. As the oldest sister, she liked to demonstrate her maturity. She complemented her words with an adult face, one that could last only a moment on a young girl. Although only eight years old, Viorica had the mannerisms of a young woman. That's what my mother used to say.

"I understand very well, Viorica. Are you helping your mother with the household?" Uncle Joseph sat between her and me, and smiled to her.

She nodded with pride as she thought of her importance in the family.

"Viorica, please be a darling and help your sister Rosy sit in her chair." My mother gave her a kind smile as she prepared the table.

Rosy, about five years old, expressed her hunger by eagerly tapping the fork on the table.

"Rosy, please stop that." My father chided in a kindly fashion.

"It's comforting to see that the family hasn't lost its spirit!" Uncle Joseph noted.

I sat quietly in my chair. My family said that I was a taciturn baby and preferred to watch events unfold around me.

"Yes, at least we have spirit!" My mother smiled as she scurried from the stove to the table. "I'll serve the children first so we'll be able to eat without too many interruptions."

Uncle Joseph tousled my hair. "You are adorable, Shuly." I'm told I was his favorite.

He held a teddy bear in front of me until I eagerly reached for it. Of course, he pulled it back just as my fingers came within an inch of the bear's tummy, and he did so repeatedly. But he gave in and I became the happiest lad in all Romania.

"Now, give me back the bear," Joseph asked in feigned sternness.

I didn't want to. I clutched it to my chest.

"He'll not give it back," said Maurizio, my seven-year-old brother we called Motzu. He returned to his bowl.

"Let's see." Uncle Joseph was planning another approach. "Shuly, *please* give me the bear." Uncle Joseph opened his arms. "Pretty please?"

I looked at my uncle's gentle eyes and handed him the bear.

"Thank you."

Later my uncle told me that he was quite surprised that I gave him the bear that night. I suspect I was as well.

Joseph held the bear for a few moments as I stared at my former possession with great interest. I wanted it back, and waited patiently. But my patience was limited and after a few minutes I started to wiggle restlessly in my seat.

"Here is the bear, Shuly, it is all yours. Thank you for letting me hold it for a while." Joseph laughed and I felt relief as I clutched my friend to my chest again.

"Thank you for the toys, Joseph." My father sliced a generous portion of pumpernickel bread and handed to Joseph. "How is life in Alba Julia nowadays?"

"The usual. I am working long hours hauling goods from town to town, but I am not complaining."

"Good to hear. How is your wife and Yanosh?"

"They are well, thanks. Yanosh is almost fifteen now and he's found a job in a hardware store. He wants to go to the university one day, so he is saving his money."

"Good for him." My mother smiled as she held out a serving dish. "Have some potatoes, Joseph."

"And my wife is doing well at home. She likes to be there when Yanosh comes home from work. The weather is getting colder but no worse than last year."

"Oh yes, it's getting colder here also." My father sliced himself a piece of pumpernickel. "Did I tell you the story about what happened last winter?"

"I don't think so."

"Ah, that was quite a day. It was about the last week of February. The snow was so high one morning that we couldn't get out of the house through the doors."

"Really?" Joseph imagined snowdrifts around the house.

"We couldn't! We couldn't!" Rosy jumped in. "We had to crawl out through the tiny attic window."

"Indeed," continued my father, pleased with Rosy's dramatic contribution. "The snow was so thick and deep that the door simply couldn't be opened. And as you've heard, the attic was our only way out."

"Yes, and I got a nasty scratch while crawling out," Viorica said. She proudly raised her arm for all to see the red mark near her elbow.

"It's healed nicely, dear. It'll be completely gone soon." My mother's voice was soothing. "We didn't have wood for heating or cooking. Here, Joseph, have some chicken soup."

"Thank you, Hermina."

"We had to walk quite a way out to the woods to find some dry branches under the snow. The kids protested that it was too cold and the wood was too heavy."

"But we made it." Rosy's cheeks reddened as she laughed. "Papa always says that we were very brave that day."

"Yes, you were." My father smiled. "We returned home, shoveled the snow from the walk, and took our wood inside. Then we gathered around the fireplace and felt the heat slowly spread into our bones. You never forget the relief from the cold, the crackling wood, and the amber flames darting about."

Maurizio dropped his fork on the earthen floor. "Yes, we cried." He murmured shyly, his voice trailing off to silence.

"Well, I am sure my brother has raised his children to be brave and devoted." Joseph smiled to all of us and raised his glass to the air. "To the brave Rittman children!"

"People say this winter will be the same." My mother sipped slowly from her soup. She didn't take any of the stew for herself yet. She was waiting for everyone to have enough before she took a single spoonful.

Joseph rested his spoon on the table and assumed a serious look. "And how is the household doing this year?"

My father nodded quietly at the inevitable question and released a long sigh. My mother looked downward.

"Not so well, I take it."

"Not so well at all," my father sheepishly admitted. "The restaurant is small and not in a good location. Too few customers. We live day to day here."

"I understand." Joseph nodded consolingly. "Solomon, you remember my suggestion, I'm sure."

"Yes. . . ." my father's voice was halting. "But I didn't find time to discuss it with Hermina."

I'm told it was more that he avoided finding the time. My mother had lost a baby boy just after Motzu, and the event left her with the need to be near her children at all times.

"What is it?" My mother stopped eating. She looked to my father, then my uncle.

"Dear," my father started hesitantly. "Joseph and I discussed a way to help the household – only temporarily."

"Look." Joseph believed in straight talk, even at the dinner table. "Our house in Alba Julia is roomy. We have only one child and he is already out on his own." His voice trailed off. "Catalina's life is empty. It would be no trouble."

My mother didn't fully grasp where Joseph was going, though she had suspicions.

My father placed an arm over her shoulder. "Hermina my love, times are hard right now. I am never sure we'll have enough food on our table. Joseph's wife needs a child in her life, in her home."

The room fell silent. The children looked at one another anxiously. They thought they saw my father's eyes mist up. There was no doubt about my mother's.

"I suggest that baby Herman come to live with Catalina and me – only for a few months." Joseph spoke softly and sympathetically.

"No!" My mother frantically took me in her arms and pressed me to her heart. "Shuly doesn't go anywhere! I need him. He doesn't eat much anyway. We will get by. We always do." Her lips trembled, perhaps as she realized the weakness of her arguments.

"Dear, it is only temporary. Only for a few months until things turn around." My father's smile was clearly forced.

"No, I say! I can't give up Shuly. He needs me." My mother began to sob, making the children all the more frightened.

Rosy, Viorica, and Motzu remained silent. They didn't understand fully but they sensed a great change was about to come over the family.

Joseph continued. "I'll send him to good schools. I'll teach him my business. I'll take him with me to markets. My wife will take care of him like her own son. The name Catalina means *pure*. Shuly will have Yanosh watching over him like a big brother."

My father spoke more firmly than before. "Remember, darling, only last week we didn't have enough for food. We got by on cabbage but there wasn't enough for everyone."

My mother rocked me in her arms, not listening to the men's words. I was silent, enjoying the motion that reminded me of my rocking chair. She finally spoke. "My baby stays with me!"

My father looked into her eyes. "Remember, we went hungry for a few days. Only stale bread. It was just last week."

My mother lifted me and looked into my eyes. I was too young to know what all the fuss was about. I at first giggled and held my teddy bear. Then I looked at my mother and was struck by her tears. I could feel her anguish. I sent my hands to her face and she burst into tears.

Uncle Joseph held a morsel of bread before me. I took it and chewed it with the few teeth I had. My gums enjoyed the stimulation and my hunger waned for a while. I'm told I was always hungry.

My mother wiped her eyes.

"He'll always have enough nourishment – bread, milk, fruit, and vegetables. He'll play on a wool rug in winter, a lawn in spring and summer." Joseph put his hand on my mother's shoulder. "Hermina, I am only suggesting this for the boy's good. And it will help the rest of you too. This is not forever, and besides, I am family. Consider this an extended vacation in Alba Julia for your little boy."

"Ha!" my mother laughed bitterly. "You always had a way with nice words. I guess you're right, though. You are his uncle. Anyway, I am sure when the kids grow up, they'll love to visit you and Shuly."

"And they will always be welcome." Joseph gushed. "I'm their uncle. Right, children?" He turned to the three children that sat at the table.

"Yes, we want to visit Uncle Joseph too," Viorica said, with a superior face.

"Yes, me too!" Rosy chirped as she held Motzu's hand.

"Dad, what about me?" Motzu asked longingly.

"We will all visit Uncle Joseph, of course. Maybe in the spring." My father joined his brother in law making the matter less trying.

"Yes, we'll all visit in the spring. Then Shuly can come home." My mother clung to this thought. Then she lifted me again to her eyes. "You hear me? I'll bring you home in only a few months. Do you want to go with Uncle Joseph? Do you?"

I sent my little hand and touched my mother's face. She closed her eyes and treasured her baby's touch. Tears streaked down her cheeks and I gently wiped them. I didn't know exactly what was going on, as time and distance meant little to a small child. I felt my mother's anguish, though.

I looked into my mother's eyes, hoping to convey, "No need to be sad, mama. I'll always love you. Always."

My mother held me and forgot where she was. It was just mother and child in the world.

Yes, I was told that it was a very hard moment for my mother and father. I of course do not remember all these events and conversations. I was much too young. But my brother and sister never forgot the scene and they recounted it to me many times over the years we had together. It was the fall of 1931. I was not quite two.

Joseph took me with him that night and my mother couldn't sleep for few weeks. Although she knew that I was in good hands, her heart ached for me, every moment, every day. She counted the days to the visit to Alba Julia when she would bring me home.

The spring arrived and my family arrived at Uncle Joseph's house. I'd grown nicely and become a toddler. Uncle Joseph took me to a baby pageant and I won first place. I had better clothes and a large yard to play in. Aunt Catalina took care of me as though I was her own. My cousin Yanosh loved me like a brother and played with me every day.

Pleased with what they saw, my family decided to leave me with Uncle Joseph and Aunt Catalina for a few more months. Next visit they'd take me home, or at least that's what they thought.

At the end of the summer Joseph and his family brought me to visit my family in Focsani and a joyful reunion followed. But again, when it was time to leave, my family felt it best to let me go with them.

A year passed and then another. I never returned to live with my birth family for many years, and even then it was not a long stay.

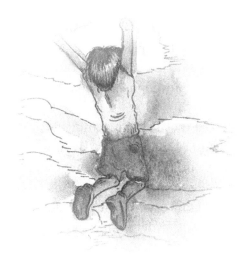

A NEW LIFE

L IFE WAS GOOD IN ALBA Julia, all things considered. I attended a Romanian public school and from a young age I loved sports, especially soccer. My aunt and uncle spent a considerable amount of time with me, and I relished every moment. We were not a very religious family; we only observed the high holy days such as Yom Kippur and Hanukah.

Yanosh, my cousin and big brother, was much older than I, and helped my uncle with the business. He also attended high school at the same time and started to work several hours a week in a car shop. I had a family and enjoyed life.

It was a delicately beautiful spring night in the year 1937 when Catalina picked me up from my violin lesson. Uncle Joseph was already home and so was Yanosh.

"What a nice surprise to find you home early, dear." My aunt kissed her husband. "I'll start dinner."

"Young man, how went your violin lesson today? Will you play something for me?" Uncle Joseph loved music and was pleased to hear me grind away on my fiddle.

I'd studied violin for the past year – private lessons twice a week. My instructor was a young woman named Anka who taught at the modest conservatory in Alba Julia.

"Yes, of course. I'll play your favorite music."

"Oh yes, a Beethoven sonata." Joseph sat in his armchair and prepared for an impromptu concert from a young prodigy, of sorts.

I removed my student violin from its worn leather case. It was an old instrument that Uncle Joseph got for a good price at one of the trade fairs he worked. I cherished that violin and always kept it dust-free and lightly polished.

I placed the music book on the stand and opened to the Beethoven section. I'd played that piece countless times and mastered it, at least as much as a young boy could. I didn't really need the score in front of me as I knew it by heart. Aunt Catalina sat next to her husband and they closed their eyes. I placed the violin's base to my chin and the music of Beethoven and Herman Rittman filled the room. Rich tones and timbres came from the resonant wood and reverberated off the paneled walls as my small hands darted about the strings. Music and love flowed in generous portions.

As I finished the piece, the last reverberation came to an end and I looked over to see my aunt and uncle leaning lovingly against one another.

"One more, please," my uncle softly requested.

Accustomed to calls for encores, I launched into another Beethoven sonata and once more music and love filled the room, if not the entire house.

"Come here, my boy." Joseph clasped his hands on my shoulders. "You played beautifully. I could listen to your music all day and all night."

Aunt Catalina kissed me on my cheek and sighed. "You did amazingly, Shuly. I love you. And now, I must prepare a dinner for the young virtuoso and his audience.

I beamed with joy and pride.

Yanosh came in from work. "Did I miss your performance, Shuly?"

"I'm afraid so, but there can be another one after dinner."

"Good news. Shall we play checkers till we eat?"

I carefully returned my violin back to its case, and we opened the wooden checkerboard and placed the disks on their squares.

"So, what did you do today before the concert?" Yanosh asked me.

"I played with Yuri and Fritz at the park."

"Very good. I was in the public library reading about airplanes. They're being built more and more in Europe."

"I hope you become a pilot one day."

Everyone in the family knew that Yanosh loved airplanes and everything connected to them. It was all that he talked about. My hope for his future was the same as his.

"Dinner is ready," Aunt Catalina announced.

Aunt Catalina was an outstanding cook. She had mastered several traditional dishes of Central Europe, none more so than beef goulash with spiced potatoes and sauerkraut. The town's bakeries and grocers accented our meals. Desserts were not outside her expertise. When in season, local cherries and strawberries graced our pies. In colder days, we nonetheless enjoyed cakes and cookies, often chocolate ones.

After dinner, we sat in the living room. Yanosh and I played board games while Joseph and Catalina discussed their days and events in the town and beyond. Although I concentrated on toys and games, I listened to my adopted parents and occasionally heard them speak in worried voices, though never going into detail. One night there was an especially portentous conversation, which I partially understood.

"I think it would be wise to make the move, dear. It will be good for us. It will be good for Hungary too." Joseph drew from his cigar then blew the smoke toward the ceiling.

Yanosh and I had heard talk of moving from Romania to Hungary, but it was only talk, much like visiting the countryside or buying a boat – nice to talk about but unlikely to occur. My uncle wanted to move to Oradea, about 200 kilometers southeast of Budapest, where he hoped to get a position in the Hungarian army. As an honored veteran of World War I, he had credentials and connections, and while our lives were comfortable there in Alba Julia, they would be all the better in Oradea. Besides, he sensed war was coming and wanted to help. War . . . that night was perhaps the first time it made its presence felt in my life.

Aunt Catalina worried about the move's effect on Yanosh and me.

"They have friends and rhythms here. Removing them from here will be quite hard on them."

"I know, but it will be better for them in the long run." Joseph looked out the window. The night was dark and chilling autumnal winds rattled windows and shook tree branches. "War is coming and if I'm in Oradea I'll be able to rejoin the Hungarian army, probably as a major. That will mean greater pull and security than a Romanian tradesman has."

"Are you sure they'll promote you? You have no assurance of it."

I pretended not to hear or to be involved, but I could hear everything they talked about. Yet, I didn't worry. Maybe it was due to a child's nature. They say that children simply don't have a sense of stress.

"They need every man in the army, as was the case in 1914. I hear from people that they accept anyone that is interested."

"I am afraid, Joseph." I watched my aunt grasp his hand. "It is still a war. What if something happens to you?"

"No need to worry, my dear. Bullets passed near me in the last war without touching me. I had a special talk with them!"

It looked to me then that Catalina didn't share his assurance or humor. Joseph looked at her and smoothed his mustache. "We've been discussing this for months now and it's time to seize the moment. Tomorrow I'll start the process."

Yanosh and I continued our game of checkers.

Catalina took a deep breath. She didn't approve, but wives accepted their husbands' decisions in those days. Later, she regretted her silence – and the seemingly insignificant move to Oradea. The city would soon change from Romanian to Hungarian rule, and in time the people of Oradea would come under the administrative control of Nazi Germany.

I was running through the streets of Oradea with school friends. I held my arms out to my sides, pretending to be a combat airplane. I made roaring noises as I flew at great speed through busy stone streets. My two friends chased me, also making the guttural sounds of great fighter aircraft. It was 1942. The war was on and boys played war. I was twelve and no different.

It was winter break. The upcoming winter looked like it would be a very tough one, or so my family said. It was already freezing outside, and a layer of snow covered the city. Winter was beautiful in the city of Oradea. The pine trees and streets were covered with snow, and there was joy everywhere. You could smell the roasted chestnuts sold from pushcarts by enterprising lads on just about every corner. Some were caramel coated and their scent traveled along with the nuts themselves, filling the nostrils of passersby and enticing them to make a small purchase on the way home.

Stores stayed open late, their window fronts brightly lit by candles and decorated with sleds, elves, and wrapped gifts. Carolers entertained homes and enjoyed a sampling of cider. People walked home with Christmas trees in tow.

The bitter cold barely registered on us as we soared down the cobblestone streets and engaged in dogfight after dogfight. The engagements took us down to the city center where government buildings, gracious parks, and a towering cathedral stood out from the shops and houses of Oradea.

Just as we were oblivious to the cold, we were also blissfully unaware of details of the war that was raging only a few hundred miles to the east. Romania and Hungary had invaded the Soviet Union. I hasten to add they did so in concert with their ally in chief, Germany – the Third Reich. In the last few months government buildings were draped in bright red flags, the centers of which had swastikas. I thought their size and colors looked ridiculous in the snow.

I changed the trim on my wings until we neared the stonework around the fountain, which was iced over, the water turned off. Nonetheless, it was an ideal landing area after a wearying patrol accented by victorious engagement after victorious engagement.

"A perfect landing!" I exclaimed proudly. Fritz and Yuri came in shortly after I did, their landings discernibly less well executed than my own, at least in my estimation. The three of us had heard countless war stories since the conflict started in June of 1941 and we recreated them each day and dreamed of them at night.

"I'm tired," Fritz panted.

"I'm hungry," Yuri added.

"Me too, but I don't want to go home," I said. We caught our breath and looked at how red our faces were. The official buildings towered above us, the Nazi flags billowed slowly until a sudden gust picked them up forcefully and spread them out like ship sails. They struck me as having both power and evil. It was the bright red, I suppose. Their motions seemed eerie and menacing. But the day was too enjoyable to dwell on it.

"I think those flags are beautiful." Yuri wiped his nose on his coat sleeve as he stared up.

"Father doesn't like the flags here in our town. He says they don't belong here and they're no good for us." Fritz spoke with great seriousness, probably emulating his father's expression as he repeated his words.

"I'm not sure just how I feel about them." I paused for few seconds as I tried to put my jumbled thoughts into words. "They remind me of circus banners . . . but they also have something scary about them too. I don't know exactly why."

"Why aren't they any good for us?" asked Yuri, still preoccupied with his runny nose.

"I don't know. Father just says they're not."

"What is it that's bad about the red flags of Germany?" I was searching for help on why I felt unease.

"Father says that the Germans want to control our government. They tell them what to do – and they fly their flags here." Fritz shrugged his shoulders. "I don't care. For me it doesn't make any difference."

"I also heard my father talking about the Nazis," Yuri added. "He said that they are taking over all Europe."

"Is that good or bad?" I asked.

"I don't know. Anyway, what does it matter? It's not like we are going to get toys and sweets from them."

We all laughed.

"Yes, it's a shame that we can't get sweets from the Nazis." I spoke with a measure of irony I didn't fully understand.

"Then we would like them better!" Fritz joked.

"We just have to tell them that!" Yuri suggested. "Maybe we should ask them!"

"Good idea! Maybe they'll give us things." I liked the idea. Ah, youth. The appeal of the preposterous.

"There are two Germans right there." Yuri pointed toward two soldiers coming out of a government building. "Let's go ask them." I think underlying his yen for gifts was a boyish sense of mischief.

"Good idea!" Fritz was in.

Driven by inquisitiveness, mischievousness, and abandon, we ran toward the soldiers. We ran so fast that we almost bumped into them. We soon saw their swastikas armbands and ambivalent sentiments coursed through me.

"Careful, little men!" One of the soldiers cautioned. "Why all the rush?"

"We're just playing. Do you guys have any candy for us?" I asked straightway and summoned a charming smile usually reserved for neighbors. We all spoke German as well as our native Hungarian. There were Germans everywhere even before the war, as national boundaries were far from strict.

"Candy? You boys want candy?" The other soldier laughed and tousled my hair. "And why do you think that we have candy? We are in the army, not the sweets business."

"I don't know. I just thought I'd ask." I made my smile wider. My two friends took the cue.

"Well, you know something?" Our eyes brightened. "I happen to have a chocolate bar." He removed a bar wrapped in paper and handed it to me. "But you'll have to split it among you three."

"We will! Thank you very much." I broke the chocolate bar into three pieces and handed out the portions.

One of the soldiers leaned down to speak to us man-to-man. "So what brings you fellows here?"

"We're playing air combat." Yuri smiled shyly.

"Air combat? Against who?" asked the second soldier in a friendly manner.

"I don't know . . . against the *bad* guys."

"And are you winning?"

"Yes."

"Well then. We are the good guys. So you three must be with our *Luftwaffe*."

"Yes." The second soldier joined in the lesson. "The bad guys are the *communists*."

"And the Jews!" added the first soldier.

I remained silent. The meaning of the words hit me and although I was young I could sense something malevolent. I knew I was a Jew. I went to a Jewish school at times, and we observed the faith's holidays. We celebrated Shabbat on Friday nights, though we were not especially religious.

Fritz and Yuri attended public school, and knew I was Jewish. They too fell silent.

The soldiers recognized the sudden change and it soon dawned on one of them. The moment of international benevolence was gone. One asked in an icy voice, "Are any of you three communists or Jews?"

Nervous, even frightened, we all shook our heads immediately, and that eased the tension. They became affable once more.

"*Gut*. All is well then." One of them laughed and concluded the meeting. "Enjoy the chocolate and always remember: stay away from communists and Jews. They're no good for Germany or Hungary."

We scurried away, our fear easing the farther away we got. We reached the frozen fountain where our planes had been refueled and rearmed for the next patrol.

"I told you the Nazis are not good. Just like my father said." Yuri looked back and saw the soldiers walk down a street away from us. "Good. They're gone."

"Right, the Nazis are no good," I agreed, "but German chocolate is excellent!"

They chuckled as they ate the last of the treat.

"What is their problem with the Jews?" Fritz wondered.

"I don't know, but who cares? We got their chocolate. Now, let's get back to play." I spread my arms out in pre-flight.

"I am going to be a big combat plane, fighting the Nazis." Yuri spread his arms and ran into the large grass area where patches of brown grass asserted themselves from the snow.

"Me too," Fritz followed him.

"I'm with you guys!"

I returned home late that night. We got caught up in our play and didn't notice the hour. When I arrived, Aunt Catalina was knitting in her rocking chair. I sat near her and she pressed me close, not mentioning my late return. She was more forgiving than Uncle Joseph, but I sensed something was amiss.

"Sorry for being late," I said after a while.

"Oh, that's fine. Tomorrow is Saturday anyway. So tell me, Shuly, how was your afternoon? What did you do?"

Her smile was forced. Behind it there was clear unease. I looked into her eyes and knew something was very wrong.

"I played with Fritz and Yuri in the park."

"They are fine boys, and good friends."

"The best. Could we have them for dinner again, maybe next week?" I felt a special pride with my friends over – pride over our home, the repast, and my guardians.

"I think we can see to that." Her reply was positive yet imprecise. She continued knitting and her look of worry returned.

"Is something wrong, Aunt Catalina?" I asked carefully, as a young by wasn't supposed to inquire about adult things.

"Oh, I don't know." She nodded and continued her knitting.

"What is it?"

"You won't understand, Shuly."

"Please tell me."

"Oh. . . . It's about your uncle. I'm worried."

"Why?" The idea of something being wrong inside my family was completely foreign. All was well inside the dwelling. Troubles were outside.

My aunt caressed my head. "You are so caring. We're so fortunate to have you with us, Shuly."

"What has happened with Uncle Joseph?"

She held an inward debate on what to say. "We moved to Oradea to be on the Hungarian side of Transylvania. Your uncle is deeply loyal to Hungary. You know that he served in the Austro-Hungarian army during the last war."

"Yes, he's told me many times."

"He was an officer then and he was hoping that in Oradea he'd be able to obtain a commission in the Hungarian army, above his rank in 1918."

"Yes, I know. He told me that too."

"But nothing will come of it. The Hungarian army doesn't want him."

"Why?" It astonished me that someone as smart and fit as Uncle Joseph would not be wanted in the army or in any other organization. Many of my friends had fathers, uncles, and brothers who were in the service. Why not my uncle?

Catalina caressed my head soothingly, at least as much to console herself as me. "It's because of the Germans. They don't like us and don't want us in the army."

"What do you mean *us*?"

"They don't like Jews, Shuly. They *hate* us."

I instantly conjured the memory of the two Germans bearing gifts.

"But why?"

My aunt just shook her head. "I don't know, love. I don't know. It's nothing new in Europe."

I sat silently, trying to comprehend this, and not knowing what to say. Many thoughts crossed my mind. Thoughts about the past and about the future. Our future. What does it mean to be a Jew? Why don't they like us?

"So what will happen now, Aunt Catalina?"

"Well, I don't know. He's very upset and doesn't sleep at night. I hope he gets over this anguish."

The door opened suddenly, startling us. It was Uncle Joseph.

Aunt Catalina immediately went to him and took his coat, as wives did then. "How are you, dear? I'll start dinner."

"I am well, thank you." He gave her a kiss and approached me. "And how are you, Shuly? How did you spend your day?" He pinched my cheek and looked lovingly into my eyes.

"My friends and I played in the park." I smiled and hugged my uncle.

"Did you hear the rumors, dear?" Joseph sat in his chair – men had their own chairs – and opened the late afternoon newspaper. "The offensive into the Soviet Union is slowing down and a major battle is building around Stalingrad."

"Yes, I heard from Bertha," Aunt Catalina answered from the kitchen, her voice a little elevated. "You know what I also heard from her?"

I sat on the couch and listened carefully, though I tried not to show it. Adults are more candid when they think children are uninterested. Bertha and her husband Rudolph were our nearest neighbors, about the same age as my guardians, with two daughters, Inga and Rosemary. They were Roman Catholic and good friends of our family.

"What did Bertha have to say?" Joseph prepared his post-meal cigar – an item that was increasingly hard to come by.

"They want to move out of Oradea."

"Move out of here?"

"They don't like the German presence. They both think they're bringing ruin on Hungary and all Europe. They predict bad things will crash down on Oradea in the not so distant future."

"They need not worry? They're Catholic, not Jewish."

I sensed Joseph was engaging in dark humor; he too believed that ruin would come to all.

"Dinner will be ready soon, gentlemen. Yes, although they are Catholic, they simply don't like the Germans. Rudolph says that they will ruin Europe – all of it."

"I would not move out, if I was them. Rudolph has a good job at the train station, and they own their home. They will get by." He returned to his meal. I looked at his face. He tried to seem casual, as did my aunt. It was an effort to keep me at ease, yet apprise me of the situation.

"Bertha thinks that we should move far away from here." Catalina said quietly, her eyes cast downward.

"We're not going anywhere. This hatred of Jews will not last. Such things come in for a while, then go away like the tide. When it goes, I will be able to serve in the army once more. So, we shall stay."

I listened carefully to their conversation. More so than ever before. Germany, Hungary, Jews. . . . I was beginning to understand something about the world. It was no longer far away. It was right here and it could reach me.

"Joseph, there's talk of the Germans treating the Jews in Poland quite harshly." Uncle Joseph kept eating. I think he'd heard the talk too. And now, so was I. "The Jews are put in work camps. I hear worse things too."

Catalina voice quavered. What are these "worse things" I wondered?

"Nonsense! The world cannot go along with this . . . this –"

"Anti-Semitism." Catalina finished the sentence.

"It can't continue for long. It has to stop at some point." Joseph was confident and a little annoyed by Catalina's display of emotion. "We need not worry too much." He finished his dinner and dabbed his mouth with a cloth napkin. "Europe is civilized, Catalina. We are all educated human beings who have been taught science and reason."

I looked over to my aunt. She didn't believe him.

"Yanosh is getting married to Adina, Shuly." My aunt told me one day when I returned from school. "He will be moving into a new place with his wife soon." She wiped a tear. "I can't believe it. My little baby is already a grownup and going to leave us. Are you sad, Shuly?"

"Yes, I am." I hugged my aunt to comfort her, though I wasn't truly sad. It all seemed normal. A young man grows up, marries, and builds a new home with his wife. Yanosh was fifteen years older than I. Nonetheless, he took me under his wing as a close brother, though at times I must say he was like another uncle – teaching me, mentoring me, showing me the way. So he and Adina were to tie the knot and live in an apartment not far from his workplace. Uncle Joseph had hinted that marriage wasn't far off and that he thought it a good thing, a proper thing.

I kissed Catalina on the cheek and said, "Yanosh has a job and now he'll have a wife. They are happy together. I am happy for them."

"Yes, I know. I am happy also, Shuly. But I look at him even now and see a boy of your age, running around the park and getting into mischief. Oh . . . I'll miss him."

"He'll live near us. We'll visit him and he'll come visit us."

Catalina treasured my concern for her. "Of course. You are right. This isn't the end of the world. He'll be right here and I will be able to walk to his apartment and hug my big boy."

"Exactly."

"And besides, I have a little boy still. You'll stay with us many years. Won't you?"

"Yes. I promise!"

"Well, this is the best news that I could have today." She gave me a long kiss and hug.

"Hello, everybody." Yanosh stepped in more merrily than usual and patted my back. "Mama! Let me hug you. And how are you, Shuly? Did you play soccer today?"

"Not yet. I am on my way to the field. Are you joining us?"

"I'd love to but I need to start moving some belongings to my apartment."

Catalina's heart sank on those words. She bravely recovered. "Are you boys hungry? Do you want something to eat? I made potato soup."

"Yes, thank you, mama. Potato soup would be wonderful." He exaggerated the affect in his voice to console her, I believe.

"Good, I am going to warm you a bowl then." She scurried to the kitchen with new purpose.

Yanosh turned to me. "So how are your soccer talents coming along, Shuly?"

"I do well. I am on the school team and play every day."

"And your violin?"

I looked at the kitchen to make sure that my aunt wouldn't hear me. "I love the violin . . . but I love soccer more. Sometimes I skip violin lessons and play soccer." I whispered, knowing that Yanosh would keep faith.

"Ah, that's fine. I love soccer too, and I wish I had more time to play with you. Maybe on the weekends you and I can play."

"I'd love too." My eyes sparkled with joy.

"I'll miss you, Shuly."

"And I will miss you."

There was a moment of silence as I think we both realized that life would not be the same again.

"Well, I need to start packing clothes and books. Do you have time to help me?"

"I'd love to help you but my friends are waiting – soccer time." I smiled shyly.

"Off you go then."

We hugged longer than usual. I hid some tears and turned to the door. "Got to go. See you later, Yanosh."

Yanosh looked after me. "See you later, Shuly."

Yuri and I met at the field as a light drizzle began to fall on Oradea. We were disappointed that there weren't other kids our age to play with us. We made the best of it and played against one another for two hours until we were soaked with rain and sweat and our shoes and socks were coated with mud. To kids, this of course was great fun.

It was Yuri's turn to challenge my goalkeeping skills on a penalty kick. He closed in, craftily faking one way then the other before booting the ball. It flew high in the air and directly toward the goal. I stooped momentarily to better my leap, my hands and fingers extended their fullest. Despite my valiant efforts, the ball sailed an inch or two above my outstretched fingers. As I came down, I turned to see the black and white sphere hurtle into the net. Yuri made a masterful move, freezing me with lateral fakes, then placing the ball right above me.

"Got it!" Yuri leaped into the air, emulating the older boys on the high school team. "Now we are tied – one, one."

"Excellent move, Yuri!" We were both honing each other's skills, so there were no losers. We sat to catch our breath, and didn't notice when two older boys took the ball from the net and started to walk away.

"Hey, that's my ball!" Yuri called out.

They continued to walk away.

We started toward them. "Hey guys, give us the ball. It's ours."

"Who are you to tell us what to do?" The taller boy replied belligerently.

"Please, we don't want any trouble. How about if we all play together?" I offered. "We can make two teams."

"No, we don't play with Jews," one of them sneered.

"I am not a Jew," Yuri snapped back but then immediately regretted his words as I remained silent.

"Then you are playing with a Jew?" The tall boy set his eyes on me. I remained quiet as my heart raced. "Are you a Jew?"

"Yes," I replied firmly.

Turning to Yuri, he said, "Then I was right. You *are* playing with a Jew." Again the sneer.

"That is none of your business. I play with whoever I want." Yuri was becoming angry.

"No, you cannot. Don't you know? No one plays with Jews. They are filthy – and *evil*."

I remained quiet. The boys were older and bigger and things were getting nasty.

"Let's go, Yuri." But Yuri was upset and likely to get even more so. He had a temper and was always one to stand up for a friend.

"You will not tell me who to play with! Now give me back my ball!"

Without any warning one of the boys punched Yuri in the face. He fell to the ground, his nose bleeding badly, crying in pain. I ran to help but the taller boy tripped me and kicked me in my stomach. I lost my breath.

The older boys kicked us repeatedly. All we could do was try to fend off their kicks and call for help.

"Hey, what's going on there?" We heard an adult voice from a way off.

The two boys stopped kicking us as he approached. It was the maintenance man who tended to the field every evening – Bernard, a man well-liked by kids and adults alike. In fact, we'd often ask him to try to kick past us as we played goalie, but he'd beg off saying he was too old.

"Leave them alone!" Bernard shouted as he trotted over to us. The boys ran away, of course. We got up and brushed the grass and mud from our shirts. "Don't ever come here again," he shouted to the boys. "If I see you here again I'll call the police."

"Thank you, Bernard. You saved us. They'd have pummeled us badly. They said it was because we are Jews," Yuri explained.

"What's the world turned into – boys doing such things." Bernard shook his head. "It is all because of our government. They allow this sort of thing. Now go home and clean up – and stay away from those crazy kids. If you can."

As we left the field we saw Bernard grumbling. "I've seen wars before." He looked at the government buildings in the distance and shook his head again. "I've seen wars before and I've seen what they do to people. Things will get worse, much worse."

"I am going to play on Oradea's team!" I stormed home one day after school.

Aunt Catalina welcomed me with joy, but a little puzzlement, too. "What did you say?"

"I am going to play on Oradea's soccer team!" My eyes must have conveyed my joy. "We have our first game next week. Isn't it amazing?"

"This is great news, Shuly." Catalina placed her hands on my shoulders.

I was the happiest boy in the world. Soccer was all that I lived for then. Practice with friends and at school turned me into a good player. My small stature and low weight was complemented by quickness and agility, which enabled me to move about defenses with ease.

The manager of the Oradea team visited schools routinely, ever on the lookout for promising talent. That day he watched a scrimmage at my school. I was in top form, passing well, stymying opponents, and adroitly moving the ball toward the goal. At the end of the scrimmage, the manager asked my school's physical education coach if I could play on the city's youth team. The coach approved and I was in heaven – and it must have showed when I came home that day.

"I am already scheduled for my first practice today, Aunt Catalina."

"Wait a moment, Shuly. Have you forgotten your violin lesson?"

I had indeed forgotten that detail and my face became less happy.

"Oh, that's fine. You can miss one violin practice. Go play your soccer."

"Thank you, Aunt Catalina, you understand perfectly. Off I go to get changed." I ran to my room to get into my practice uniform.

Over the next weeks I practiced diligently with the Oradea team. The others on the team were much better athletes than my friends and schoolmates, and this sharpened my skills. My passing, agility, and kicking became much better. Athleticism came at the expense of musicianship. This saddened my aunt and uncle but my dedication to soccer gladdened them.

"You'll be a renowned soccer player one day," Uncle Joseph used to say, though only half-heartedly. "I was hoping more for a musician, but an athlete is good too."

"It's what he likes. That's what's important." Aunt Catalina's words were just as resigned as her husband's were.

I promised them that I'd continue to practice the violin, and I did – just not nearly as often before, and not nearly as enthusiastically.

My guardians attended my games and were proud of the trophies and awards I took home. The soccer profession beckoned.

———————————⌒———————————

In the fall of 1943, with the war still raging to the east and getting closer, Oradea was playing against the team from nearby Debrecen. At halftime I sat briefly with my aunt and uncle and tried to catch my breath.

"You are playing well, my boy," Uncle Joseph smiled proudly.

"Thank you. This is a tough game. Good players. The best we've seen yet. But we're up to it. We'll come through in the second half. You'll see."

"I have no doubt." Aunt Catalina reached into a basket. "Here, I brought food for the three of us."

"I'll eat after the game. We have to keep light for the game – coach's orders." I hopped up and down, first on one leg, then on the other – much to their puzzlement. "I'm trying to fend off the cold, dear ones."

"Well, I hope I will not offend my young nephew if I nosh a bit right now. All you're hopping about has made me hungry. Ah, salami!" His eyes lit up as Catalina handed him a slice wrapped in butcher shop paper.

A man dressed in a suit approached us. People dressed well at public events back then, but there was something out of the ordinary about him, something official and unfriendly He was not there to watch the game.

My uncle stopped eating.

"Are you the Davidovich family?" The man spoke without any greeting – and quite gruffly. He was in a suit that even a boy could see was inexpensive and didn't fit well.

"Yes, we are. I am Joseph Davidovich and this is my wife Catalina. This is our son, Herman. He plays on the Oradea team. It is our pleasure to meet you. And with whom do we have the honor to speak?"

Uncle Joseph extended his hand, but the man made no effort to shake it.

"Your son will no longer play on Oradea's team, as of this very moment."

My aunt and uncle looked at each other in confusion and disbelief.

"May I ask why? And who are you?" Uncle Joseph was upset but controlled his emotions. I think he knew what was coming.

"My name is Arthur Bodor. I am with the Iron Guard and I am now an assistant to the mayor. Jews are not allowed in official positions." He then glared at me. "You are forbidden to play another minute on the team."

I cringed. Anti-Semitic boys were one thing, but they were mere nuisances. This man was with the Romanian fascist group that was influential in Oradea, even though the city was now under Hungarian rule. The Iron Guard, also known as the Archangel Legion, was an ultranationalist movement that hated communists, foreigners, and Jews. Bogor had the Iron Guard, city bureaucracy, and the gendarmerie behind him. And they were all increasingly hostile to Jews. The signs were there over the last few months.

"Take your son and leave the field." Bodor gave his orders, added a menacing glance, then turned and walked away.

"Let's go, Joseph." Aunt Catalina was alarmed, close to tears.

Uncle Joseph was stunned. The Jewish community of Oradea had experienced anti-Semitism for the past few years, and probably more and more of it, but our family had fortunately not witnessed any. Now there was this Bodor fellow from the Iron Guard coming up to people and issuing orders.

"Wait!" I protested. "I have to help the team. It's only halftime."

Uncle Joseph shook his head. Anger not far beneath the surface. "Shuly, my boy, you heard that man. I'm afraid it's over. You can no longer play for the city."

"Can we stay here and watch?"

Aunt Catalina silently stood and stepped up to the back row. Uncle Joseph and I soon did the same.

Halftime ended and teams went back on the field and resumed the contest. Minus a key player, Oradea was at a disadvantage, if I do say so myself. I looked on in frustration as our offense sagged and Debrecen moved the ball closer and closer to the goal before one of our players made a defensive play. Nonetheless, a trend was clear and after twenty minutes or so, Debrecen scored. There was nothing I could do.

Our coach looked into the stands and saw me. During a penalty he came up. "Herman, here you are. I was looking for you all over the sidelines. What are you doing here?"

Uncle Joseph found the words. "I'm sorry but a man from the mayor's office was here and he forbade our boy from playing anymore."

"What?" My coach was annoyed. "I do not know that fellow and I don't care what he says. This is my team and I say who plays and who sits."

"He is with the Iron Guard," Uncle Joseph added.

My coach became silent as he heard the name. Not far beneath my coach's silence was anger.

"No! I'll not allow those crazy people to ruin my country or my team. Herman, go back on the field. I'll call a time out immediately."

My heart rejoiced. Aunt Catalina was alarmed, though.

My coach tried to assure her. "Do not worry, madam, this Bodor fellow is not here now and I don't care what he said anyway. Herman is playing and that is a fact." He then looked around.

"He left after he ordered us to leave," Uncle Joseph replied in an unsettled voice.

"Then all is well. Come and sit near me, in case he comes back. And Herman, get down there now!"

I returned to the field much to the appreciation of my teammates and even some people in the stands, besides Joseph and Catalina of course. Energized, I played well. I'm fairly sure I scored a goal.

Things were changing in Oradea. The war was going badly and people began to look warily and even angrily at Jews. I felt it. Friendships ended, neighbors stopped speaking. My aunt and uncle felt it. The entire Jewish community of Oradea felt it. On May 3, 1944, the deputy mayor of Oradea decreed that Jews must wear the Star of David.

The atmosphere became increasingly worrisome as the weeks passed. Uncle Joseph smoked more and more cigars, even though they were from cheap Balkan tobacco. Aunt Catalina tried to knit but her anxiousness made her hands too imprecise. Eventually, she stopped.

"We have to do something, Joseph," she announced one evening. "Jews are losing their jobs, their children can no longer go to school. Fear is everywhere. I worry for us, and for Yanosh and his young children."

I listened intently. I had little real knowledge of politics but my guardians did and I respected their views. I also picked up on unspoken things.

Uncle Joseph shook his head. "I can't believe this is happening. I served in the Austro-Hungarian army like any other Hungarian in the last war. I was on the battlefield. I suffered with my fellow soldiers. We do not deserve this, Catalina. We do not deserve this!"

"I know, Joseph, but the government doesn't care about right and wrong from the past. Many of our friends have already left Oradea. Others were deported to the ghetto. What should we do?"

That word – ghetto.

Uncle Joseph knew he had to protect his family. It wasn't a matter to be discussed; it was his decision. He looked at me and I awaited his words. He knew that the time was at hand. "We have to move away from here," he said in dejection. "Tomorrow, I'll talk with Yanosh. I want him and his family to leave with us."

Aunt Catalina wiped a tear. "I think this is the right decision, Joseph."

Even I felt a relief. Somehow I sensed that moving away was the right thing, though I didn't know where we'd go.

Uncle Joseph nodded silently. He had a downcast expression on his face. Remembering that moment I think that he already had a feeling that events had gotten out of hand.

And it turned out he was right.

We woke up a few mornings later to the sound of loud knocks on our door. A commission of three arrived: a civilian, a government clerk, and a gendarme – the term used for the national police. Their faces showed determination, and no sign of compassion.

"You're moving out. Pack up only a few things."

My heart sank.

Uncle Joseph didn't ask any questions. He knew he had to accept the power of the authorities. He had seen the gears turning for weeks and now this – knocks at the door and stern orders. Aunt Catalina was alarmed.

We soon learned that we were being sent to the Oradea-Mare ghetto.

TO THE GHETTO

WE DIDN'T HAVE TIME TO pack many things. That was by design. We filled suitcases quickly and stuffed things into bags – bedding, clothing, groceries, cooking utensils, and a kilogram or two of coal. I packed only two small bags.

Is this all that we'll be able to save? I thought uncertainly. Will I be able to continue playing sports? What about my friends? When will I see them again?

As we quietly gathered our things, I saw tears in Aunt Catalina's eyes. So sad for all of us. We had to leave behind family mementoes from many happy years together. All the family events, graduations, games, friends, and relatives had to be left behind. Uncle Joseph voiced what we all were thinking. "We'll be able to return one day and find our house just as we left it."

He packed books into his valise. I watched quietly. A proud, patriotic man was trying to maintain dignity and self-respect, confidence and faith. Today I know that he did it for us. So we would not be afraid. So we would persevere and believe that all this would be over one day.

We were distracted by unusual, disconcerting sounds from the street. Old people, young people, and small children, all with bundles on their backs or in their hands, slowly followed luggage-filled carts as they were herded along by gendarmes. It couldn't have been more than thirty meters from me and I saw anguish and despair on every face.

I recognized school friends and their families. I reflexively waved to them but the dreadful occasion asserted itself on me, as it already had on them. I lowered my hand and felt warmth drain from my face. There was a solemn crush of newly dispossessed people on the street in front of our house, and we were about to leave that house and join them.

Aunt Catalina was distraught. Uncle Joseph returned to packing. The meaning of all this penetrated me, and I became devastated as well. Waving and smiling were parts of childhood that had to be left behind.

Two more gendarmes arrived. They rifled through our luggage then rudely told us we had taken too much. They took inventory of the valuables left in our house – carpets, candlesticks, furniture, and the like. They ordered my aunt and uncle to hand over their wallet, purse, and money. Uncle Joseph complied immediately, though not completely.

The final moment arrived. I felt sick as I watched Uncle Joseph close the door and hand the key to the gendarme, who tagged it and placed it in a box with many others. And that's how our home was taken away from us. That home meant safety and security for me. I spent my childhood there. It was my safe harbor. No more.

Would we ever be back? Would we ever see our home again? I wiped a tear, and am close to doing so now. That moment is embedded in my being as one of the hardest ones in my life.

Another humiliating moment came. The police demanded our rings, necklaces, and other jewelry. Here Uncle Joseph protested but he was shouted down by angry references to laws and decrees. Aunt Catalina could no longer keep it in; she broke into inconsolable tears. She was so frail.

For the first time that day I felt wrath – a powerful anger focused on the gendarmes who were humiliating my beloved guardians. But I understood that my anger would worsen matters, and I held back from any rash act. Yes, it could be worse. We trudged down the street with our luggage and bags, three more people in a long line of people on their way into the unknown.

All I could see around us was misery, pain, and despair. People didn't look at each other, only straight ahead. Broken human beings abruptly stripped of home and hearth and pushed into the streets. One after the other, occasionally hearing words of encouragement, we followed those ahead of us, like blindmen in a dense fog. The sight of our sad convoy pushing forward filled me with grief.

As a fourteen-year-old, I felt better with my guardians by my side. I knew they were afraid also but there was solace and strength in being with family. I was intermittently jarred by the thought of being separated from them – a thought I'm sure must have passed their minds and the minds of everyone on that march. There no longer were homes, belongings, laws, or decency. I imagined we were walking back into the past before there were such things. The strong took from the weak, then told them to march away.

I have the strange recollection that it was a beautiful day. Spring … the spring of 1944. The scent of foliage and blossoms coming forth occasionally reached my nostrils, leaving me with not a sense of beauty, but of paradox – a cruel, unforgivable paradox.

More and more people were herded into the march. The residents of this street and that avenue endured the same knocks on the door and gruff commands that we had an hour earlier. Just ahead I saw a shoddily built brick wall with a wooden and metal gate. Behind them was an old, rundown part of the city – dilapidated tenements, broken pavement, debris strewn all about. We walked out of the graceful city and into the cheerless Oradea Mare ghetto. I shivered as I walked through the gate. I had entered a kingdom of evil. Aunt Catalina took my hand and gently pressed it. I felt better.

The crush quietly trod down the streets of the ghetto in a long line, gendarmes alongside. We saw people along the streets and in doorways. They looked thin, sickly, and dispirited. It slowly dawned on the newcomers to the ghetto, that these famished people had been herded into the walled-in district some time ago, several months or more. We were looking at ourselves in a few months.

Aunt Catalina clutched her husband's arm tightly and held me close to her. She and many other women sobbed softly as they filed down the stone streets.

I looked behind us and saw Yanosh, his wife, and small children. It was not the time to call out or wave. I was glad to see him and I was sorry to see him. I wished he'd gotten out of the city and hidden in the forests or found refuge in a sane part of Europe. Yanosh appeared calm and brave. As I looked about I saw many such displays among the marchers. None among the onlookers.

Gasps and whimpers came from the front. In a few moments we were struck by an overpowering stench. It wasn't garbage or sewage. Those were common enough odors in cities then. This was something else, something that seemed putrid and sweet at the same time. Off to the left were piles of an uncertain nature, maybe a meter or more high. I soon identified shoes, arms, and then thin gray faces.

"Oh, my God, those are dead people!"

Aunt Catalina's horrified voice spread fear and nausea through the marchers. The onlookers, I could see, were accustomed to the sight. Some had probably stacked them on the sidewalk themselves.

"Dead people . . . dead people lying in the streets," I murmured, trying to comprehend what I saw.

"Yes, those are dead people," he said in low tone. "Just continue walking, Shuly. Let's go."

I'm sure the sight was shocking to my uncle. He'd seen dead during the last war. He nonetheless continued with the march.

Many of the corpses were in grotesque positions, legs dangling toward the pavement, stiffened arms pleading upward for an answer. I saw the corpse of a young girl with a small doll clutched in her hands, and thought it must have been placed there by a grieving parent. That was all I could stand. I looked straight ahead.

Gendarmes stood on corners and directed people down side streets to their new dwellings. There was method in the madness. It became clear that the ghetto was badly overcrowded, despite the decreases in population that we'd seen lining the sidewalks. There were newcomers last week, we were coming in now, and more would be arriving soon. The ghetto was about twenty square blocks and it was horribly overcrowded. There were probably four times as many people in it than in any district its size in Oradea.

We were happy that Yanosh and his family were assigned to the same tenement building as we were. They'd be living one floor above us. We had another family living with us.

The apartment was quite small – a one-bedroom apartment one might call it today. There was a twin bed for my aunt and uncle; the rest of us made do on mildewy mattresses stuffed with old straw, which filled the room with a rancid odor.

The floor was covered, to some extent, with cracked black tiles. Mold had accumulated between most of them. The walls were bare concrete with dark stains as the only accent on the drab gray. A few ramshackle pieces of furniture were here and there, probably left behind by the poor souls who lived there before us. We later learned that the buildings, indeed the whole district, had been declared unfit to live in by the city. Somehow, the city deemed the buildings fit for at least some people.

Aunt Catalina was distraught. "How can we live like this, Joseph? I can't do it!"

My uncle could provide no answer. "How can they put fellow humans in this squalor? Even in the war we had better billeting."

"A gendarme said it will be only for a few months," said the father of the other family assigned to the room. "My name is Jacob and this is my wife Wilma. These are our four children."

"An honor to meet you. I am Joseph Davidovich." Uncle Joseph, ever polite even in these circumstances, introduced us as he would at a restaurant or school. He looked about the room and shook his head. "I never imagined that it would be this bad. I never imagined anything like this."

Jacob looked at him quietly. "No one did, Joseph, no one did."

"Well, let's get settled." Jacob spoke spiritedly. The task of organization brought purpose. I think he even smiled. "We'll be here for a few months, and after that we'll be taken to a better place. There are work camps where there are military-like barracks with beds and cooking areas."

"Yes, I'm sure you're right," Uncle Joseph said.

Thinking back on those days I'm amazed how well we managed. We found boards and nails and made shelving to store our meager belongings. We took the malodorous furniture outside to freshen it as best we could. We made sleeping arrangements for women, men, and children. There were two creaky wooden beds which were allocated to the oldest women. I slept on the floor near Uncle Joseph in one room. He wanted me near him. He felt obligated to my parents in Romania whom he'd convinced to let me live with him.

We gathered what food we had and subsequently scratched up and stored it in a small pantry used by everyone in the building. We established a roster of items and times for cooking and cleaning. We also had to regulate the use of the bathroom. It is amazing to witness humans in dire conditions. We helped each other. We supported each other. We comforted each other.

Sometimes I'd think about my friends in the old neighborhood. They were only a few kilometers away, yet they were in a different world – a world of tidy houses, parks, and hope. In their world, gendarmes held up the law kept them safe. In mine, the gendarmes enforced edicts and kept us walled in.

Uncle Joseph said that within the next few days the gendarmes would assign us jobs. That was welcome news. I liked the idea of having a job, just like a grownup.

After a few weeks, a five-member Jewish Council, or *Judenrat*, was nominated. Having our own leadership had a calming effect. The *Judenrat* oversaw day-to-day life in the ghetto and tried to solve problems related to food, public sanitation, and administration. I worked for the *Judenrat* by delivering messages to people. This enabled me to hear discussions and decision making – quite a feat for a young lad.

The council comprised a number of Rabbis, doctors, and lawyers –prominent men of the Jewish community of Oradea. Each I believe tried his best to make life more endurable in the ghetto. (The same cannot be said of Jewish councils in other ghettoes, I later learned.)

We established a dining hall in the ghetto. Since many people arrived unprepared, the community mess was their only food source. Soon, a few thousand people were eating there on a daily basis. The number of needy newcomers was ever on the rise, and supplies quickly diminished. The old kitchen became too small for present needs and a new one had to be set up. Young men were recruited to build another kitchen in an abandoned laundry building. We worked an entire day to construct another dining hall. Our reward was free food.

Within a few weeks food reserves were troublingly low and the *Judenrat* addressed all residents. Everyone was asked to hand over all food beyond what they needed for the next few days. We complied. (Our family still had food from the house.) I put together several jobs which paid me in food. Uncle Joseph managed to barter things. We never had to rely on the communal dining hall.

The gendarmerie ordered the construction of a hospital, and a building adjacent to our dwelling was selected for the site. We made simple beds from planks and benches. Bedclothes and sheets were gathered from the population. There were many doctors among us and they pooled their medical equipment. All this we did ourselves. The gendarmes helped not one bit. My family, owing to our proximity, helped a great deal.

I was fortunate to get a janitorial job in the hospital, which of course was never short of patients. Many people had arrived in the ghetto seriously ill and in those living conditions, the number of sick people rose. Furthermore, many people suffered grave injuries while under interrogation by the gendarmerie. I saw many people who'd been through the process and there was clear evidence of torture – some of it so harrowing and painful that people chose suicide.

After finishing my janitorial duties I helped sick people eat, wash up, and go to the bathroom. I became what we'd call a practical nurse. The patients grew fond of me as I was attentive and cheerful.

Many patients suffered from stomach problems, pneumonia, and other illnesses related to the living conditions. Hygiene was difficult to maintain. Water was scarce, both in the hospital and in the ghetto in general. Sometimes the authorities would shut off the water in the entire district for hours, and sometimes for days. The same with electricity. People had to relieve themselves in the open, which led to a terrible stench hanging over the ghetto.

Plumbers had to work hard to open clogged pipes. People got sick, lost hope, and died.

Amazingly the spirit of life remained with most young children and teens. We simply adapted to the new life style and didn't complain much. There was enough family strength and community awareness that we felt it our duty to help wherever we could.

A few weeks after we arrived the ghetto was packed – no, overpacked. One day the authorities levied about two thousand people for labor service. They were ordered to equip themselves with food and clothes to prepare to leave for work the next day. Yanosh was among them. We hoped he was off to a better situation.

I was cleaning the hospital when the news arrived. The commander of the gendarme regiment in Oradea had taken command of the ghetto. At first we didn't think it meant much. What else could be done to us? But new rules were published. The gendarmes handed out new decrees and posted them on corners. New degradations. The decrees determined bedtime, waking time, and even mealtimes. The ghetto was to be quiet as a graveyard from nighttime till dawn. Anyone caught outside was subject to being shot on sight.

And so a deathly silence fell upon the ghetto at eight pm. The authorities shut off the electricity and darkness descended.

I used to go up to the roof and look around at the lights of Oradea. The air was better up there. I could hear in the distance the sounds of automobiles, trains, and occasional shouting and laughter. Rather than being resentful, I thought it wonderful that there was life out there, not far from me. I imagined myself again running down the streets to the park with my friends. I closed my eyes and breathed deeply.

THE DREHER

T HE GENDARMES TOOK CONTROL OF the Dreher-Hagenmacher brewery. At first we didn't care. We didn't use the old brewery for anything. Nothing had been brewed there for decades. It was an empty building with broken windows.

One day, my friend Isaac arrived at the ghetto hospital. "The brewery is being turned into an interrogation center."

"Interrogation center? For what?" I kept sweeping the floor.

"I don't know. But I hear they think we're hiding money."

"There's no money inside these walls. It can't mean much."

My reply was dismissive, glib, and wrong.

Isaac was right. The Hungarians were obsessed with the idea that we had left valuables with friends or neighbors for safekeeping just before being marched off, or that we had valuables with us inside.

They decided to get the information through torture. The "Dreher," as it came to be known, was transformed from an abandoned factory into a dreaded prison.

Every day, a few dozen people were ordered to appear there for interrogation. The gendarmerie sent a messenger to bring them in. We called the messenger for our district "Jonah." Old men and women, young people, and even sick people were taken there. Many old people died during the procedures. Survivors spoke of the gendarmerie as the Hungarian Inquisition.

We learned that the gendarmes had been trained by the Nazis in the ways of torture. The descriptions were horrible. I had bad dreams from simply hearing them. Jews were stripped of their clothes then beaten with leather belts, whips, or iron rods. Some had their heads smashed against the concrete walls. Other were strapped to a chair and given powerful surges of electricity. Parents had to watch helplessly as their children were beaten.

People heard loud music being played from the old brewery. The gendarmes wanted to hide the screams.

More and more people were called. People were terrified at the prospect of being summoned to the Dreher. Some chose suicide over going there.

My family and the others sat around the rickety wooden table. It was Friday evening and we were about to conduct a Shabbat – a rite that had become more important to us since entering the ghetto.

A white cloth lay across the table. Aunt Catalina had washed it as best she could that morning. Each of us sat in front of chipped and cracked stoneware. Two challah loaves, bought that day from the makeshift bakery, emitted a homely aroma that offered hope. A silver Kiddush cup held a few ounces of watered-down juice. Somehow my aunt was able to get hold of some poultry and the prospect of chicken broth enticed us all. Jacob's family managed to put together a passable salad composed mainly of boiled potatoes.

Aunt Catalina lit two candles, and Uncle Joseph raised the Kiddush cup in the air and recited the Kiddush prayer. He then poured small portions of the juice into every cup. He blessed the bread and gave everyone a small piece sprinkled with salt.

"Shabbat Shalom!"

"Shabbat Shalom!" came the reply from all in the room.

"Are we hungry?" Aunt Catalina asked in a cheerful voice.

"In good times we took the Shabbat for granted. Now, it reminds us that life goes on and that there is always hope." Uncle Joseph spoke cheerfully as he stirred his soup.

"I hear that soon we'll all be out of this horrible place," Jacob said in equal cheer. "We'll be sent to work camps where there will be better food and housing."

He looked tired. Jacob was perhaps fifty but looked older. He'd been a metal worker outside but inside he worked any type of work just to bring home some food.

"Yes, I heard that also." My uncle nodded.

A knock at the door caused everyone to stop eating and look around.

"Who's there?" Uncle Joseph spoke in a strong voice, conveying authority.

"It is me – Jonah. I am sorry, very sorry. But I was sent to pick up Jacob."

Everyone knew Jonah, or of him. He was the gendarmerie messenger and that night Jonah was sent to bring Jacob to the Dreyer.

"It is the Shabbat, Jonah. Go away and come back on Sunday." Uncle Joseph rebuked him through the still closed door.

"You know I can't do that." Jonah's voice was timid. He didn't want to lose his job.

Jacob stood and spoke, his gray beard moving in concert with his words. "I'll go. I am ready to go. Anyway, I don't know anyone that has money. I'm sure that they'll release me soon enough."

His family was devastated. They looked to us for help but knew we were as powerless as they. I wondered if he could survive. No, I was sure he couldn't.

Uncle Joseph went to the door, but didn't open it.

"Jonah, I told you it is the Shabbat now. Now please go and come back later."

"I don't want to do this but I'll be severely punished if I don't bring him back with me. I am very sorry. You know that."

"You could tell them that you couldn't find Jacob. Come back on Sunday. He'll be ready then." Uncle Joseph looked at Jacob, his family, and us. I knew he was doing what he could, but I also knew that he couldn't do a great deal and that there were risks to interfering with gendarmerie business.

After a few moments of painful silence, Jonah spoke. "I'll be back to take Jacob on Sunday."

We listened as his footsteps faded in the distance. There was rejoicing, then crying. But Jacob wouldn't have it.

"Let us be jubilant! I just earned another Shabbat. Are we going to enjoy our soup or are we not?"

His face was sooty from the day's toil. His coat was threadbare, his shirt lacked a few buttons, and his toes I knew stuck out from his right shoe. Yet in his eyes there was life and hope, if only for a while.

We resumed our meal with even more enthusiasm than before the knocks came.

Jacob spent the rest of his reprieve with his family. They hugged, they sang, they prayed. I watched in amazement. I knew that in a few hours he would leave our dwelling and walk down to the Dreher.

Jonah returned early Sunday morning. Tactfully, without actually saying goodbye, we bade farewell to Jacob.

"We'll see you soon, Jacob. Be strong."

Jacob was ready to go. He smiled and gave kisses and hugs to us all. "It's fine. I am already old."

But then sadness came over him.

"Don't let what goes on here remain untold."

I doubt I was the only one who was taken by his words.

We never saw Jacob again.

PERSEVERING

A MAZINGLY, PEOPLE PUSHED AHEAD. THOSE of us who were in our teens tried to find any reason to be happy, and we usually found one or more. Some of us were fortunate to find old friends among the ghetto population. I soon found Isaac, who was my age, Sergei, who was thirteen and had his Bar Mitzvah just a few months earlier, and Haim, who was the oldest at fifteen.

One night we sat outside and talked about our former lives. "I miss eating my mother's cooking," Haim said wistfully. We remained quiet. It wasn't simply out of nostalgia. Haim's mother had been taken to the Dreher recently and come back badly injured. Her wounds became infected and there was nothing the hospital staff could do but clean the injured areas and change the dressing as often as possible. Haim's father, we knew, had told the family to prepare for the worst.

"I miss playing with my friends from our block," Isaac lamented. He was the most outgoing of the group and had the busiest schedule on the outside.

It was my turn and I had to think for a while. What *did* I miss the most? Yes, of course, there was the obvious – a normal life, normal food, a bed and security. But what would I really enjoy to do right now?

"Soccer." I said in a hushed tone. I don't think I even meant to speak out loud.

"What?" Isaac didn't hear me.

"*Soccer.* I'd love to play soccer. I was getting good at it."

"I also like soccer." Isaac stood as though the coach was sending him into the game.

"I never played soccer . . . but I'd love to try." Haim was not the most athletic kid in Oradea.

"Splendid. However, we have two problems." Gears were turning in my head. "First, we need a place to play. The ghetto doesn't have an open space for even a small soccer field. Second, we don't have a ball."

What Haim lacked in athleticism, he made up for in resourcefulness. "Well, as for an official soccer field, we simply can't get one. We barely have enough space to live. But who said that our soccer field has to be official size? It can be smaller. Half or even one quarter of the city's field."

"Exactly!" I was the one to stand this time. "We practiced on small fields. We even practiced on corner lots . . . well, when we were smaller."

"We can play in the yard near where we do laundry. We'll clear out the garbage and make space." Haim was in top form.

"We still need a ball." I brought us back down to earth, so we did a little more thinking.

"My cousin Grisha knows a way out of the ghetto," Isaac announced warily.

"You don't have to speak so low, Isaac. No one hears you besides us," Haim chided.

We all knew Grisha. He was younger than we were, about twelve years old. He took things harder than we did and was always looking for ways to get around them. There should have been more us like Grisha. I'm surprised there weren't. Nonetheless, we thought it both fitting and delightful to cause as much trouble as possible for those vicious gendarmes. As young Jews, it was our duty. In fact, we'd have been pleased to die in the cause. Oh, but what did we know of death?

"He knows a way out. I'm sure of it. I've seen him many times bringing food from the outside. He sneaks out, pretends to be a local beggar, and gets money for things. I can ask him to buy us a soccer ball."

Haim voiced elated approval. I, however, was more cautious. Risking your life to get money for food was one thing. Food is essential and there was precious little of it in the ghetto. But risking your life to get a plaything, that was quite another. Still, I wanted to play soccer badly and my youthful zeal overwhelmed what little caution a young man has. I came up with justifications. Soccer would make us healthier. It would cheer us up and the others inside the walls as well.

Two nights later, after promising Isaac we'd never divulge the secret, he took us to a distant part of the ghetto perimeter where the barrier was made of dilapidated wooden planks, probably by hurried, uninterested work crews several months ago. I looked for a hole in the barrier as best I could in the darkness which was only barely broken by a streetlight on the outside. Isaac pointed downward then carefully pulled away a few crates, revealing a hole.

"A tunnel! A passage to the outside world!" I gasped as though seeing Jacob's ladder or the Red Sea about to open. "Did Grisha dig it himself?"

"It isn't really a tunnel, just a small hole under the wall," explained Isaac. "I went with him once. It was very scary because there were gendarmes patrolling just outside. They almost heard us. My cousin is very brave!"

"I don't know about this. . . ." Haim mumbled.

"Where did you go?" I marveled at the idea of going off into a world forbidden us.

"Nowhere really. I was too scared." Isaac shrugged his shoulders sheepishly. "I crawled back inside immediately! Grisha will be back soon, hopefully with a gift for us – a gift from the people outside the not-so-solid walls of the Oradea Mare ghetto. We'll have to wait – and we'll have to wait very quietly."

"How long?"

"How should I know!"

It was summer, yet the night was cool. We sat near the wall and tried to keep warm. Several times we held our breath as we heard the heavy footfalls of gendarmes just the other side of the wall. We imagined ourselves bold soldiers on a secret mission for our nation.

Suddenly, we heard lighter footfalls, then scratching noises. Someone or something was coming from under the wall through the secret crawlway. We froze in fear. To our relief, and delight, Grisha's dirt-smeared face emerged out of the darkness. He too was frozen in fear for a moment on seeing three dark outlines standing above him, even though he was expecting us.

"It's you guys! I brought you some treats."

He handed candy and we became the happiest boys in the world.

"That's all I could get. Try as I did, I couldn't get money, only candy. Maybe tomorrow I'll have better luck."

We had a wonderful evening all the same, and there was the promise of things to come the next night or the one after it. It was something that broke our tedium and brought something to look forward to, small though it was. It was more than a ball; it was resistance to the gendarmerie and Nazi-leaning Hungary. It was the only way we could fight back and assert who we were. We imagined the Reich fearing us.

Grisha became one of us – the youth resistance of Oradea. Grisha snuck out of the ghetto almost every evening and he was expert at scooting under the wall without being detected. No one outside the ghetto suspected that he was Jewish and many people gave the poor ragamuffin a little food or money. He offered to take us along with him but we were too scared to do so, even though we were a year or so older. There were limits to the valor of our resistance movement.

On nights that Grisha didn't go outside, he tagged along with us. We learned that his father was a schoolteacher and now worked in the dining hall as a helper, and that his mother died at a young age from an illness. He had no brothers or sisters. He had a strong, free spirit and hated the gendarmes. He expressed to us many times that he would fight them if he weren't so young and small. We admired his spirit.

One night, as with many before, we waited for his return from the city. We sat quietly listening to routine sounds of the city streets across the wall. All of a sudden we heard whistles and shouting. We sat still even though fear was surging through each of us. The yelling got louder and we could hear people running on the other side of the wall. We looked to the hole and suddenly saw a soccer ball, then Grisha!

"Here, guys. I was a little luckier this night."

We heard commotion just over the wall. Grisha suddenly lurched backward, pulled by someone. A gendarme began to shout to his colleagues.

"Quick, get away from here," Grisha shouted.

All three of us grabbed an arm, a hand, a shirt and began pulling him inside, but there was now more than one gendarme. One or more were pulling him out, another was kicking him or clubbing him with a rifle and calling him a "dirty Jew." Grisha grimaced and gasped with each blow. Judging by the sounds and the gasps, the blows were getting harder. Suddenly, Grisha fell silent, his body became still. The gendarmes stopped pulling, perhaps thinking their work was done. We pulled him inside.

"Grisha! Grisha!" Isaac called to his cousin.

Grisha stirred. He was clearly in great pain. He couldn't stand or walk. I suspect now that he had quite a few broken bones. We stooped over him, knowing the gendarmes were several blocks away from an entrance and we had a few minutes until they arrived.

"It hurts . . . so much." The brave lad grimaced but held back from crying. "I got you a soccer ball!" He managed a faint grin.

"Grisha, let's take you home to your father. He'll help you." Isaac started to lift him up.

"No, it hurts too much. I can't walk. Just let me rest here. Stay with me. Please. . . . I knew it would happen. The gendarmes spotted me . . . I was too fast." Another faint grin. "I ran so fast."

We were helpless to do anything for him.

"You know, I do believe I'm going to die now." He spoke softly and without fear. "I feel it."

"No, Grisha. Hold on. We'll take you to the hospital. Let's lift him, guys – now." We followed Isaac's urging but again the pain was too much for Grisha.

"Just let me be, just let me be." A few tears formed.

We all started to cry. He was gravely injured but unable to be moved. Broken bones, internal bleeding. The gendarmes had beaten the poor boy so badly, he would die right there before us.

Grisha lifted his head. "You guys play. I wish I could play with you." He feebly extended his hand and shook each of our hands.

We promised to play and held his hands. He lay back and whispered, "I'm so tired . . . so very tired."

He closed his eyes and left us.

We all sat near his now lifeless body, sobbing quietly. There was no time for lengthy grieving. We carried the body to his father. Grisha's trials in the Oradea Mare ghetto were over.

Isaac, Haim, and I met every night. I'd stowed the ball away in our apartment. There wasn't much to talk about. We were sad, we were angry, we wanted to get back at the gendarmes. We knew, however, that their capacity to get back at us – and at the whole ghetto – was enormous. It wasn't for a week until I brought the ball out one night.

"You know," Isaac said late that night, "Grisha wanted us to play soccer."

"Yes, he certainly did," I replied, holding the black and white leather sphere. "He most certainly did."

"Then we have to play," Isaac concluded.

Haim nodded. "If we play, we have a small victory over those who killed him. We have purpose, we have life."

"And Grisha will have life, with every step," I added. "Tomorrow, we'll meet at the field behind our building. And we'll play with Grisha's ball."

And that's what we did. We played soccer a few times every week, even in the summer heat and rain. Other kids in the ghetto joined in, and together we had fun and we had youth – all within the walls of the Oradea Mare ghetto.

ALEXA

A NURSE URGENTLY CALLED FOR MY help as I was sweeping the floor in the ghetto hospital.

"I need your help with a patient this minute!"

The hospital was overcrowded, the staff overworked. Helpers were called in for emergency help from time to time and with little notice.

She hurried me to a room where several people lay on makeshift beds. On a small table were several vials of medicine.

"We don't have too many of these left," she said as she plunged a needle into one of the vials and slowly drew the serum into the glass tube. "Please hold her arm tight. She simply doesn't like shots."

The shot was administered without much of a fight and the woman lay back calmly.

The nurse was quite lovely – twenty-five or so, with brown hair.

"What's your name, young man?"

"Herman"

"Your age?"

"Fourteen."

She smiled and shook her head.

"Aren't you too young to work in a hospital?"

No response came to mind. What did I know of what was normal?

"Well, thank you for your help, young man."

She turned to the patients and I watched. She listened to them, spoke to them, got to know them and their infirmities. I was fascinated by her. I was smitten by her.

A few days later she noticed that I was watching her perform her duties as I changed bedding. She looked to me.

"Do you have family with you here?"

"Yes, my aunt, uncle, and cousin." My voice must have conveyed shyness.

"Where are your mother and father?"

I told her the story of my family's poverty in Romania and my informal adoption. When I asked of her family, she saddened.

"I arrived here with my mother and father. My mother died three weeks ago from liver disease. My father is here in the hospital. He is in a coma and there's little expectation he will come out of it."

She sat on a wooden chair and collected her thoughts.

"My father was a plumber. He was summoned to work on a leak, and I went with him. Two gendarmes saw us and began to beat my father. Harder and harder. I called for help but of course no one would interfere with the gendarmes. One of them looked at me and I saw such hatred in his eyes. No plea could have stopped him. The beating stopped and my father has never returned to consciousness."

She cried for a few minutes, then looked about the crowded room with sleeping patients.

"What's the use of all this? We're all going to die one way or another – starvation, disease, beatings. I hear we will be sent to place far worse than this. Some say it's idle rumor, but I'm beginning to believe it.

I hadn't heard the rumor. I'd only detected gloom and despair and dire forecasts. I wanted to cheer her. I told her the war might be over soon and we could all return to our homes outside the walls.

She laughed bitterly.

"How can we wait until the end of the war when we have so much to survive here? How long until the Russians get here? One year? Two years? Ten? Haven't you seen people die here?"

I told her I had indeed seen people die here. I just thought the day would come when we would return to our homes.

Her eyes left mine.

"Well, I have a plan."

After making sure the patients were asleep, she reached into a pocket and removed a small cloth containing a vial.

"This is my escape plan, Herman," she whispered. "A few minutes after I take this, I'll be in a better place."

She saw my discomfort.

"What do I have to lose? What do I have to look forward to?" She said cynically. "One day I may be taken to the Dreher. What do you think they'll do to a young woman like me? Or one day a gendarme will see me and take me away somewhere."

She was right. It was all true. I nonetheless urged her to keep her spirits up.

"I don't think I'll survive this, Herman. I don't see a way out other than this one."

She tapped a finger on the vial.

Knowing she might take her life at any moment made me worry. Many people in the ghetto were opting for that way out. I tried to be close by while I performed my duties. She performed hers, professionally and kindly, though with discernible gloom hovering over her.

We spoke briefly every now and then – about our families and schoolings. When she spoke of boyfriends, I must confess to pangs of jealousy, which very much surprised me. She enjoyed running and competed in track events in school. Naturally, I brought up my soccer talents.

———————

One evening I was cleaning up in the room of her comatose father. She sat on the bedside, desolation written on her face.

"He'll never wake up. I'm all alone in the world."

I told her that I was with her and was always willing to help. She smiled and said that someone my age was the one in need of help and comfort. I countered manfully by saying that I knew how to make my way in life. It was becoming true.

Sadness returned to her face. In fact, it intensified. She stood near her father's bed and looked outside into the darkened, empty streets of the ghetto. I expected her to cry but she was worrisomely calm. I thought of summoning help in case she reached into her pocket.

"Your father may recover."

"No, Herman, he won't. And even if he did, what prospects would we have?"

She shook her head quietly. Then took the vial from her pocket. I could see the fluid move about in the dim light. Should I run to her or get someone from the station down the hallway?

As she opened the vial, I moved toward her. But someone reached her before me and knocked the vial from her hands. It fell on the floor and shattered, the contents spreading out across the cold concrete.

"No, Alexa! No, I say!"

It was her father's frail but nevertheless stern voice. He'd raised himself from his deep sleep and was now lying back down. She immediately turned to him.

"Papa! You're with me! Are you hungry, Papa?"

"Not hungry."

A doctor arrived and looked at the man and welcomed him back to the world, but he motioned for the doctor to leave.

"Alexa, my child . . . never . . . never even contemplate such a thing."

Alexa wept on her father's chest.

"You are helping people here . . . and you must continue. Your place is here. Your purpose is here, until your time comes. Promise me. . . ."

"I promise, Papa."

"Louder."

His sternness returned.

"I promise to see this through, Papa."

———————⌒———————

That night, when I returned home, I climbed to the top floor and looked at the city outside the walls. A boy pondered the ideas of purpose in life and more importantly, the importance of keeping one's word.

Alexa's father slipped back into a coma and passed away gently not long thereafter. I was in the room when she hugged him and he took his last breath.

Alexa was deported from the ghetto before I was. I thought I'd never see her again.

SOLOMON

TWO MEN BROUGHT A BATTERED old man into the hospital and made room for him. He was barely conscious and signs of beating were plain. A pair of doctors came to see to him and learned from the men that the injured man had just come from the Dreher.

"What's your name?" one of the doctors repeatedly asked. The poor man was unresponsive.

The other doctor looked at the bruises and cuts, and whispered, "Brain damage."

Neither doctor was surprised by the wounds or the diagnosis. Neither was a young boy with a broom and mop. The doctors lamented that they had no way to treat the man. The implication clear, they gave brief instructions to a nurse and left. There were so many others to see.

I put my mop against the wall and stood over the man. Dried blood had caked inside his ears. A good face, a kind man, though time and abuse had taken tolls.

"Aaron? Is that you, Aaron?"

His eyes opened slowly as he spoke. They were reddened and showed distance.

"My name is Herman. I work here. You are in the hospital."

"Aaron? What are you doing here?"

"Aaron?" I asked tentatively.

"It *is* you – my grandson! I haven't seen you in so long. I was afraid I'd never see you again, but here you are."

A faint smile relieved some of the pain on his face and in my heart. I'd seen this delirium before in the hospital, and I'd seen caring people handle the unpleasant situation.

The nurse returned to wash his wounds.

"Are you related to this man?"

"No, I'm not," I whispered. "He thinks I'm his grandson, though."

"Oh, I see. We'll hope for the best, but these injuries are very serious. Very serious."

The nurse placed a moist cloth to the man's forehead and asked his name repeatedly. Getting no response, she left.

A few minutes later he spoke again.

"Aaron? Aaron? Where are we?"

"In the hospital."

"Hospital? But why? Why, Aaron?"

"You were at the Dreher."

"The Dreher? What kind of place is that? Tell me, please."

"It's a very bad place. You were injured there. What is your name?"

"Oh, Aaron! You know my name. I am Grandpa Solomon. Don't you recognize me?"

It was good to see the trace of a smile.

"Of course, Grandpa Solomon. Of course, I recognize you."

"I missed you, Aaron. I missed you for so long. Where have you been? Where?"

"I was playing with my friends."

"Playing with your friends. I'm glad. You are a good boy."

I finished my duties in that room and was about to leave when the nurse returned. When I told her of my conversation, she wanted to know what part of the ghetto he lived in. I asked him.

"Oh . . . I don't know, I don't know."

The nurse thanked me, encouraged me to talk more with him, and went on to her next patient.

Solomon's eyes were open, the light of life was dim. He tried to speak but could not begin. So I did.

"I am here, Grandpa Solomon."

"Aron? Is that you, Aaron?"

"Yes, I'm here."

"Thank God you are here, Aaron. I want to see you. Where are you? Come closer."

His hand reached out and I took it.

"Ah, here you are. Thank you for being here, Aaron. I don't see well anymore. I am old. I forgot how old I am." He laughed softly.

"Yes, that's funny, Grandpa Solomon."

I didn't go home that night. The nurse brought me a little food and I stayed with my new grandfather. I fell asleep in the chair, despite the sounds of pain and anguish from other patients.

"Aaron? Aaron?"

"Yes, Grandpa. I am here."

His voice was steadier. I became hopeful.

"Do you remember my wife, Aaron?"

I didn't know how to respond. He continued.

"Rebecca – my wife of forty years. You loved her cooking."

"Yes, I did. A wonderful cook."

"She died not long ago, on our anniversary."

"Ohh. . . . I didn't know."

"Children are not supposed to know these things. Rebecca and I had many years together. You know, every couple has good years and bad years. We ended with a good year."

He faded.

"A good year then. I'm glad."

"She became sick . . . from an infection. I don't know medicine, Aaron. She faded every day. Like a candle, Aaron, like a candle."

I thought of his eyes.

"Aaron, I do remember the Dreher now. They beat me, Aaron. All over my body."

He tried to turn to me but the pain was too much.

"I want to tell you something, Aaron. They asked me where the money was hidden. I was going to tell them but they beat me before I could speak. So, I didn't tell them about the money in my neighbor's house. They beat me so hard. . . . I am glad I didn't talk. They don't deserve it. Oh Aaron, look what they do to us!"

"I know, Grandpa, I know."

He closed his eyes and fell asleep. I did the same.

"Aaron? Are you here, Aaron?"

There was panic in his weak voice.

"I am here, I am here."

He reached for my hand and relaxed.

"I am glad you are here, Aaron. I don't want to die alone. I know I'm going to die soon. Did the doctor tell you when?"

I hesitated. I didn't want to be anything but honest with Solomon.

"The doctor said it wouldn't be long."

"Not long, not long. I'm not afraid, Aaron. I'm not afraid to die. I'll be joining my wife. Life hasn't been sweet without her. Aaron, I want to tell you something."

"I'm here."

"I want you to have my money when the war is over. You are young. Use the money to raise a family. Help others. Give to the poor. Be good. You were always a good boy, Aaron. I trust you to do good."

"Yes, Grandpa Solomon, I will."

He motioned for me to lean down then whispered the location of the cache of money.

His hand loosened as morning broke. Solomon had died. I sat for a while, grieving for the man. I notified the morning nurse and walked home. I forgot the location of the cache before I fell asleep.

ANTON

ONE MORNING, AS I WAS walking to work at the hospital, a gendarme on horseback called out for me to stop. Thoughts of being taken to the Dreher came swiftly to mind.

"You! Come with me."

Had he seen me that night at the wooden wall? Had someone informed on me?

I looked at him. A young man, maybe in his early twenties. His uniform was clean and freshly pressed. He lit a cigarette and smiled at me. Sensing no malevolence, my fear waned. I followed behind him and we exited a checkpoint at the gate and we walked down the streets of Oradea until coming to the gendarmerie stables.

"What's your name, boy?"

"Herman."

"My name is Anton."

With that, he did something unexpected. He reached to shake my hand. I almost pulled back out of instinct. Grisha was not far from mind. Nonetheless, I wiped my grimy hand on my shirt tail and shook Anton's hand.

"Do you have brothers or sisters, Herman?"

"I have a cousin who is like a brother. His name is Yanosh. I have true brothers and sisters in Romania. But I didn't grow up with them."

"You are fortunate to have not grown up with sisters. I have two at home and they drive me crazy at times!" He laughed in a very casual manner. "I was assigned to find someone to help with the horses. They need to be cared for – and on a daily basis. Have you any experience in this sort of work, Herman?"

"No." I immediately regretted my answer.

"Oh, in that case I'm not sure you fit the job."

"No, no! I'll do excellent work. I promise to learn the job quickly and see that every mount is in the best of shape for the morning."

He noted my urgency. How could he not? He looked at my dirty and tattered shirt, my worn shoes, and my thinness.

"So you think you can manage the job then?"

"Yes, I'm sure of it!"

I saw the opportunity to get out of the ghetto for a while and learn about what was going in Oradea and beyond. I would even learn something about the gendarmerie. I'd already learned something.

"Good. Then come with me, and I'll show you around the stables – where materials are and the like."

There were about ten horses. Beautiful animals. Some chestnut brown, some shiny black. All looked strong and spirited. My job, as Anton explained it to me, was to feed, wash, and brush them in the evening, so that they would be in good shape for mounted patrols in and around the ghetto.

He looked at me. I sensed it was the first time he looked at someone from the ghetto as a human being.

"Herman?" He looked at me intently. I felt fear again. "Are you hungry?"

I nodded silently.

"Come with me then." He took me to a cramped untidy room with a desk and piles of papers. "Wait here." He returned after a few minutes with bread, beef, sauerkraut, and a cup of water. It took a moment for me to be sure they were truly for me and this wasn't a cruel trick on a famished boy.

Hesitantly, I began to eat, trying not to do so mannerlessly. It had been months since I ate a meal like this. Bread and potatoes were all we had inside for the most part.

"This is from our commissary. Naturally, you are not allowed there, but a good stable hand cannot go unrewarded." He watched me eat, studying me, puzzling over something. He released a long sigh. "You are Jewish, yes?"

"Yes."

"As it happens, my brother married a Jewish girl. Very pretty. Minna is her name. She has such a lovely family. I ate at their table many times. Wonderful people. Her father is a doctor and her mother took care of the neighbors' children during the day. Wonderful people." He looked out the window toward the walls not a hundred meters away. "When all this started, my brother took his wife and her family and crossed the border into Romania. He didn't want them to end up over there in the ghetto."

I wondered if things were better for my family in Romania.

"It is not good what's done to you in there." He looked wistfully toward the walls then to me. "Ahh, but there is nothing I can do. I am just a simple gendarme. Finish your meal. Do your work well."

I learned my duties that day, and from then on I was a regular sight at the stables, washing and grooming the magnificent beasts. Most people there ignored me or looked disdainfully at the stable boy. Anton was always agreeable to me. He made sure I'd eat reasonably well everyday. He even gave me sweets, cigarettes, and occasionally liquor, which I brought back inside to eager family and friends.

In return, I worked diligently. While stable work isn't always pleasant, it was less onerous and despairing than being a practical nurse at the hospital. I must say that the horses and I developed a certain mutual fondness. Strange and paradoxical, I know. They were the obedient steeds of the oppressors. And Anton wore the uniform of the Hungarian national police.

Also strange and paradoxical were my walks to and from work, accompanied by a gendarme or someone from the stables. I walked the streets of Oradea and saw the freedoms and normalcy of day-to-day life. The ghetto gate divided two worlds.

Every night, after passing through the checkpoint, oppression and terror came down upon me again. The gendarmes were summoning more and more people to the Dreher. It was clear that torture victims gave up names of innocent people simply to end their agonies. The gendarmes were concentrating on people thought to have had a measure of wealth before entering the ghetto. Poor people had less to fear.

Then, however, the gendarmes began to summon people at random. Suicides increased. I was fortunate to get away from the ghetto every morning and work with my equine friends.

One evening, just before work was done, Anton brought me a more generous amount of food than usual. "Here, eat." He smiled but seemed uneasy.

"Thank you. I can eat as we walk back to the gate."

Anton motioned for me to sit.

"No rush. I want a smoke before we go."

I had no complaint with that. If I had, I wouldn't have voiced it. We sat on a bench just outside the stable, the scent of horses, hay, and strong Balkan tobacco filled the summer night. I ate in a more gracious manner than the first time I was given a meal from the gendarmerie commissary.

Anton was pensive. He sat back against the wall and loosened the top button of his tunic. I had the feeling that he wanted to talk, so I waited.

"You know, Herman, I am just a simple soldier, but I have common sense." He looked dispirited. "I see what we're doing here. I know what we do in the Dreher. Have you heard about the Dreher, Herman?"

"Yes, I know about it. Many of my friends' family members have been interrogated there." I became silent, but not sensing any ire in Anton, I continued. "Many didn't come back. Others came back badly injured."

He looked up at the sky. "Yes, that's the place. That's the Dreher. A few weeks ago they wanted to assign me there. I *declined!* I said I was better suited out on the streets, on horseback." He stiffened in pride, than sank down and shook his head. "It is sickening what's done in there."

He looked out the window to the wide street leading to the ghetto and I suppose we both thought of daily events inside. I looked to him and saw sorrow, regret, and vulnerability. I saw a human with all those emotions, despite his uniform and the power behind it that was supposed to pervade him.

"I am very sorry, Herman."

I was too young and too surprised to know how to reply. Yes, Anton was always agreeable to me, but this was the first time I saw warmth in him, and remorse over what was happening to us Jews. His uniform made it all the stranger, even though his tunic was unbuttoned and he had a cigarette dangling from his mouth.

"I hope that you survive this. I hope that you and your family get through this. Still, there are worse places."

"Thank you."

I could articulate nothing more than that.

He stamped out his cigarette on the brickwork below and stood – the cue to head back to the ghetto. I entered through the checkpoint and went home. I never mentioned the episode to family or friends.

New rumors spread. The rumors were about a plan to send us to the Far East or to camps to the north. At the time we did not understand what a camp meant but it sounded better than the ghetto. Better quarters, better food, better treatment, and away from the Dreher. The gendarmes told us that we would all stay together and move to camps with better conditions. Later I realized that this was a ruse to avoid panic – and maybe an uprising. The rumors were about factories, workshops, and farms.

Uncle Joseph was heartened. "They need us to work at these camps. We will be valued laborers. We'll be treated much better there."

It all happened very fast. One day, when I returned from work, my uncle told me that a few blocks had been evacuated. The people, a few hundred perhaps, were given an hour to prepare. The suddenness and mysteriousness naturally caused concern. Uncle Joseph was uneasy. Why the rush? Why the secrecy? Everyone was asking the same thing the following day, in the dining hall, on every street corner.

The *Judenrat* asked the Hungarian authorities about the evacuations and what lay ahead. The authorities would only say that the evacuees were sent to perform agricultural work somewhere within the boundaries of Hungary. No more details were given.

The evacuations continued, still without explanation. For all the privations and horrors of the ghetto, it was beginning to have the attraction of being known and understood. That seemed better than the unknown where our worst fears created dark images.

The authorities published lists of the sectors that were next, and shortly later the gendarmes closed them off. No one could go in, no one could go out. The inhabitants were told to gather a few belongings and prepare for deportation.

After a few weeks the once densely populated Oradea Mare ghetto was almost empty. The dining hall was quiet, save for the occasional sound of a pot clanging to the kitchen floor. Those of us who were still there concluded that the secretiveness was upheld to prevent panic.

New regulations were imposed. We were forbidden to leave our dwellings except to go to the dining hall or hospital. I was nonetheless allowed to go to my work at the stables.

Anton arrived one evening to take me back to the ghetto. As always, he brought me food. I began to thank him but he interrupted. He looked anguished.

"Herman, today is your last day here. Orders from the commandant." He pointed desultorily toward the administrative office.

The day I knew would come, had come. I looked around at the stacks of hay, saddles, and gentle horses.

"So it's goodbye then. Thank you for all your help, Anton."

"Listen to me, Herman." His voice conveyed great urgency. "You have to listen to me."

I prepared for bad news.

"Soon you and your family will be placed on a train."

"Yes, I know. To a work camp. The rumor is that we will work on farms somewhere in Hungary."

"*Forget that rumor, Herman!*" It was as though he was angrily rebuking my naiveté. "You have to escape. It doesn't matter when or where. On your way to the train, during the trip, or at any other time. It doesn't matter. Just run at the first opportunity. Run!"

"I can't do that, Anton, I have to be with my family. I can't leave them."

"I know it will be hard, but trust me, you have to get away." He clasped a hand on my shoulder. "You are young. You can run. You can hide. *Do it!* I am telling you, Herman. Run away from that train. You must not reach where it's headed."

"Why, Anton? Where's the train going?"

"Nowhere good." He just shook his head. "Herman, just run away. It's for your own good." His eyes held a horrible secret and I knew he would not reveal its details. He shook my hand, sorrow and finality in every motion. "I hope the best for you, Herman."

"I hope the same for you, Anton."

He escorted me to the gate. No more words. He turned and walked away briskly then broke into a run. I never saw him again.

———————

Anton knew where the trains were going and what went on at their destination, at least in general. He couldn't tell me for fear I would spread the word and he would be blamed for the ensuing panic and resistance. Anton, a man in the detested Hungarian gendarmerie, cared for me and wanted me to survive. I'll always remember his kind heart. In another time, in another place, in another uniform, Anton might have been a great soldier.

I hope he too survived.

LAST DAYS IN THE GHETTO, JUNE 1944

M Y JOB AT THE STABLES was over, I remained with my family inside the walls. I didn't tell anyone what Anton told me. I didn't want to frighten anyone more than they already were. My friend Haim had been evacuated with his family already and the only friend that was still there was Isaac. We daringly walked at night through deserted streets. They used to be crowded with people and daily goings-on but were now eerily silent, like old graveyards at midnight.

Houses and apartment buildings that had been hurriedly emptied were all the more silent. Doors were open and they creaked disconcertingly with the slightest breeze. Pots, dishes, pillows, and toys were strewn here and there. Every block or so we'd come across bags and suitcases stuffed with belongings. There was no sense in picking through them. Isaac and I knew we'd both be gone in a few days, no more than a week.

I was asked to help in the ghetto hospital again. Naturally, I complied. Many despairing people went there for comfort. Some pleaded for a way out of what was coming.

Yanosh returned from his labor battalion and his family came to live with us. The husband and wife that lived with them upstairs committed suicide, taking poison together. They were old and unable to handle another forced removal to who knows where.

Many people dreaded the impending evacuation and hid in deserted buildings, attics, and sewers. Some had long known of holes and tunnels and chose to attempt escapes to neighboring villages. Others hopes to make their way across the border into Romania. I later learned that a few made good their escapes and that those who had hidden in the ghetto were eventually found and imprisoned by the Hungarian authorities. They were sentenced to hard labor, but they were not sent to where we were destined, and most survived.

Knowing that evacuation was imminent, and that notice would be short, we prepared for the day. We removed sheets and tablecloths and wrapped our belongings in them. Though early summer, we made sure to pack what little warm clothing we still had. Most of it was not in good repair. We also packed a few items of food. We placed the bundles near the door.

It was our last Shabbat in the ghetto. The table was not covered with the white cloth. It had been used to pack clothes and was sitting near the door. There were candles, plates and bowls, and cabbage soup. No challah, only rye, probably a few days old.

Uncle Joseph said the Kiddush over the wine and the prayer over the bread. Yanosh was with us and so were the children of the family that lived with them. Yanosh took it upon himself to take care of them. Now he had his wife, his own offspring, and two new children to take care of.

We ate our soup in silence. The atmosphere was one of hopelessness. We were on the brink of the unknown – unknown and dreaded, and increasingly so. The prospect of better conditions in a work camp or on a farm had long since faded, though our hearts seized upon the idea from time to time.

"Tomorrow we'll make our final preparations." Uncle Joseph spoke somberly. "I want everyone to pack food and clothes in separate bags."

Aunt Catalina looked at him in dismay. "Separate bags? But why?"

I too found the directive unsettling. If there was one sustaining faith for us, it was going through what was to come together.

"Because, my dear, we don't know what lies ahead. We may be separated." Over the last week or so, Uncle Joseph spoke more crisply, more authoritatively, as though an officer again, and we were soldiers entrusted to him. As though we were in a war.

Uncle Joseph held her, consoled her. Their love and caring was the essence of that sustaining faith. We all pondered the prospect that our days together were few. I hid my tears, or at least tried to.

We didn't say anything more that night. We finished the meal and went to bed. I couldn't sleep. Many thoughts ran through my mind. Where will we be in a few days? Will we be able to stay together? What will become of us?

The next day, as instructed, I packed my bag – underwear, two shirts, two pants, torn socks, a sweater, and a coat. My aunt gave me a loaf of bread, a few potatoes, cabbage, an apple, and even a piece of chocolate that she'd kept just for me. She also gave me a cooking pot and blanket. I looked at the pot and wondered what I would do with it. I came up with no answer but packed it all the same. I closed up the bundle with my uncle's old belt.

Aunt Catalina cried and I hugged her.

"Don't worry, everything will be fine and soon the war will be over." I was a mere fourteen-year-old boy, consoling my aunt, with words I didn't believe.

The evacuation continued. Our block was the only one left. Isaac and his family were taken a day earlier. There were no goodbyes.

Our day had come. I woke up early and walked the silent streets. I looked down the street and knew what would soon transpire. I'd seen it often enough over the last weeks. Shouting gendarmes, gruff orders. "You have one hour! One hour!" A long line of people, bags and bundles, sadness and fear. Then the march to the train station.

I thought about Anton. Why did he tell me to run? What did he know about our destination?

Should I run?

No, I couldn't leave my family. I couldn't leave Uncle Joseph and Aunt Catalina. They may need my help and I may need theirs.

I saw an old shoe, a tattered newspaper, a lonely teddy bear sitting on a broken chair.

Who were the owners?

Where were they now?

DEPORTATION

THE KNOCKS CAME. THE ORDERS were shouted. We gathered our bundles and walked uneasily down the streets toward the train station, the sounds of our footsteps and a crying child reverberated off silent building fronts. Over to one side there were neat rows of flowers outside a deserted house. On both sides of us were gendarmes.

Optimism came to the surface every now and then. I was leaving the ghetto and I'd soon be walking down the streets of Oradea, where I'd run and played. A better future seemed possible. Anything would be better than the foreboding ghetto. Then Anton's words would return. I walked on.

We slowed as we passed through the narrow gates separating the ghetto from the rest of Oradea. Outside, people stood on sidewalks or in windows and watched our procession. Some of the onlookers had distraught looks. A mother and a child of ten stopped and looked at us. The mother covered her face. I think she was crying. Others looked sternly, as though justice was finally being meted out before their eyes. Most, I must say, had puzzlingly expressionless faces.

At the train station, the gendarmes were supplemented by Germans – the SS. I saw tall cattle cars sitting at the far side of the platform so they didn't interfere with regular train traffic. As we neared the cars, some people rushed to be first, as though to get a good seat or more room. An SS guard gave loading instructions to the gendarmes, but they seemed to resent him and did not snap to his orders. The gendarmes, I began to think, were less brutal than these SS troops.

We were led into cattle cars. My aunt and uncle, Yanosh and his family, and I climbed aboard. We were packed in, though not nearly as tightly as on my subsequent experiences aboard what I came to call the Death Express. We were able to sit on the worn floorboards. A gendarme shouted through the closing doors, "If anyone escapes, you will *all* be severely punished." We were used to barking gendarmes so it didn't really mean much.

I was eager to know if the gendarmes would be on the train, or if we were solely in the hands of the SS. I found my way to a narrow airshaft in the cattle car and through the small opening I could see gendarmes. I announced this to the others and they were relieved. Why did we suddenly feel good about gendarmes? Perhaps it was because we had become accustomed to them and understood them. The SS might be far worse.

Uncle Joseph and Aunt Catalina kept saying, "Thank heavens we're staying in Hungary. Yes, thank heavens for that." People clung to that belief.

"I can't wait until all this is over." I looked to Uncle Joseph for hope.

He patted my back gently. "The war will be over soon, Shuly. We'll all be back to our normal lives. We can get through this. We're better off away from that filthy ghetto."

Aunt Catalina smiled and nodded.

It wasn't just us. I think most of us on the train felt, at least intermittently and briefly, that getting away from the ghetto was for the good. What could be worse?

The whistle blew. I peered out the slats and saw gendarmes and SS guards conferring. One wrote something down. An SS guard, probably an officer, motioned ahead to the conductor. With loud clanging from the couplings and a sudden jolt, the train began to move out from Oradea.

Here we go, I thought. But where to? I looked at the buildings, trees, and a dozen passengers standing on the platform. Is this the last time I'd see Oradea? Will I ever be back? I took a few bites from the black bread Aunt Catalina gave me.

Uncle Joseph was designated in charge of our car and he oversaw the distribution of water stored in a large military container. Small children had first call. Older people were allowed to spread out on the floor. Complaints were negligible. It was good to be on our way.

As we chugged along, people began to talk.

"I heard the gendarmes say we're heading for Kassa where there are labor camps," a man said as he beamed with confidence. It was Tuvya, a shoemaker, about sixty-five-years old. I took an instant liking to him, his kindness clear.

"No! We're bound for Mezotur," said another man named Nachman. "I'm sure of it. I overheard high-ranking gendarmes when I was in the Dreher last month."

We looked upon him with sympathy and respect. He noticed.

"Yes, I lived through it. I was lucky. They hit me several times with their whips, and that was it." He shrugged his shoulders. "They concluded I was no source of great wealth!"

Tuvya patted Nachman's back. "I am glad you made it. My brother was not so fortunate. He was beaten so hard that he died shortly afterward."

The car fell silent, as most of us knew someone who'd shared the same fate.

The train slowed, clanging and screeching noisily, then came to a stop. Nachman peered out from gaps in the siding and reported that our train was being put on another track. "We're not going to Mezotur now. Shame, I really wanted to go there. I have family there."

I didn't know why he mentioned his family. Even if we went to Mezotur, I sensed we wouldn't be free to move about and look up friends and family. We'd be in a labor camp of some sort and watched over by gendarmes – or by those other fellows.

With the train stopped, the summer heat and close quarters soon affected us. Water ran out and children cried. But there was nothing to do about it.

A gendarme shouted, "We're going to Kassa."

"I know Kassa! I've been there many times on business." Uncle Joseph's mention of familiarity brightened faces. "It's a small town just inside Czechoslovakia. I was there during the war – the previous one, of course."

"I was hoping to go to Mezotur. There are many chicken farms there," Tuvya recalled. "Better we remain in Hungary."

"Kassa is in a mountainous area. It'll be much cooler there," Uncle Joseph recalled. "Much cooler. We'll be there soon. You'll see."

People chatted about Kassa, the mountains, and people they knew there. I remained silent. I just wanted to get out of the car and find some water.

We remained stopped at the switch junction. The heat worsened and mothers pleaded to anyone outside for water. A gendarme gave us a bucket of water and we all thanked him. The children drank, as did we all, and the car became quiet again save for a few conversations to pass the time. Again, we came to appreciate the gendarmes.

Then the gendarme told us that we were not going to Kassa. Instead, we'd get off six kilometers from Kassa where Jews from Transylvania were being put in a camp being built right now. "This is what the SS officers tell me. I'll bring you further news as I receive it."

Uncle Joseph was disturbed, Aunt Catalina quite gloomy. Most remained silent, everyone in their thoughts. I imagined a small camp with wooden huts for us to sleep in. Green fields all around.

Uncle Joseph spoke. "They want us for labor. It's common during wars when manpower is needed. We'll be working for the army. They'll value our work and treat us well. Hard work is nothing to be afraid of!"

I envisioned outdoor work in a placid countryside then shook my head dismissively. My mind was vacillating between hope and fair so wildly.

The train at last moved out from the switching point and after a few hours, the train stopped outside Kassa. I looked out and saw the station platform a hundred meters or so away. A group of gendarmes conferred. One came to our car.

"One man gets off to fetch water."

Tuvya was our man. He went out and returned with a bucket. Some drank, some washed their faces. Tuvya trotted back for more. I admired the vigor of this elderly man.

I saw the gendarmes conferring at some length with the SS. The gendarme commander was unhappy. His face showed disbelief. Then he barked orders to the other gendarmes. They spread out to the cars and ordered us to turn in all of our valuables. Anyone who withheld anything would be executed, by the Germans. People were distraught, partly because they would lose the last of their valuables, but more because they knew they were under the control of the SS now.

We were given a sack and soon it was filled with money, jewelry, and personal goods. Uncle Joseph surrendered several watches he'd kept for bartering in an emergency. Aunt Catalina handed in the necklace that she'd been given on her engagement. She treasured it more than anything. Other people complied too, as best I could tell. Married couples wept as they placed item after item into the sack. An absolutely heartbreaking scene.

A boy of fourteen had no real valuables.

The gendarmes collected the sacks then slammed the car doors shut. "Make no effort to flee. Anyone who tries will be shot immediately."

It was our farewell to Hungary. I sat there and thought. It came to me. The gendarmes were never concerned with us. Our desperation made us think there were benign people in charge. But this was simply a delusion we clung to. The gendarmes were no different than the SS. A boy of fourteen could see that.

Night fell and we all lay on the car's floor, often in unusual positions so as not to discomfort those next to us. I found a place near the back, above which were cracks and openings that allowed me to see the night sky and its countless stars. I slept only fitfully as the train rocked about, slowed then sped up, and sounded its piercing whistle. I looked at the stars and wondered what they knew about our destination.

Sunbeams shot through the car, waking me and others. We stood as best we could, stretched our legs, and tried to work out the pains from lying on a hard floor.

"I think we're heading for Germany," Tuvya said as the train rounded a curve.

Uncle Joseph looked for the sun.

"I am not that sure."

"I think we're still heading north," said another man. "I am almost sure of it."

"Then we are heading for Poland," Uncle Joseph said. "But why Poland?"

"Maybe they're take us to Lublin?" suggested one of the women.

I looked at her and noticed an elegant dress. She spoke with an upper-caste accent that we didn't hear often in our neighborhood of Oradea. We were working class, she was higher. Much higher. As light spread, I saw her disheveled hair and grimy face with streaks formed by falling tears. She had dressed for the occasion of our deportation, and put on makeup as well.

"What else could there be in Poland other than Lublin?" she asked calmly. "I've been to Lublin. Such a *beautiful* city. You'll love Lublin. All of you." She began to laugh, more and more, then uncontrollably. "We're all going to love it there! We're all going to love Lublin!"

My aunt and uncle looked at each other sorrowfully. It came to me. The poor woman had fled into a comforting world of past visits to a charming city. She was better off there.

Another woman curled on the floor near me and said, over and over again, that she didn't want to live anymore. Others tried to help her. Many people lay listlessly on the floor.

An older boy, maybe sixteen offered me a cigarette. I didn't smoke, but I took it all the same. We had no way of lighting our cigarettes, of course, but we held on to them.

A young girl reached for my hand. I looked at her. She was about six or seven. She had long blonde hair and was clearly frightened. I held her small hand and she looked less so.

"My name is Marisha." She spoke quietly and in a friendly manner.

"Where are your parents, Marisha?"

"They both died in the ghetto. I live with the Grossman family. They are on the other side of the car."

What circumstances had brought us together. I held her hand to encourage her. I was not sure how much help I could be, though. We stood there together as the train continued its journey, occasionally turning abruptly and jarring us to one side. We were exhausted, thirsty, and hungry. Day turned to night.

The train slowed and came to a noisy stop. We sat, waiting. We could hear doors opening on the other cattle cars. Moments later, our doors were opened. Fresh air at last. I saw hundreds of people standing along the cars in the night. SS guards, snarling dogs at their sides, shouted at them and at others climbing down from the cars.

There was smoke in the air. Small particles fell from the skies. Not snow in summer. I rubbed some in the palm of my hand and held it to my nose. Soot.

"Where are we?" asked Tuvya. No one answered.

Three SS soldiers came toward us. An officer announced, "This is the final destination."

People were relieved. The journey was at last over.

The elegant lady exclaimed, "Thank God! We've finally arrived!" I'm sure she thought she was in Lublin.

I looked at the SS officer. His affable face put me at ease for a while. Maybe things will get better here, I thought.

He brusquely told us, "You are in Auschwitz."

Yes, I was in Auschwitz. It would be the first of my two arrivals there on the Death Express.

AUSCHWITZ

" **E**VERYBODY OFF! BAGS REMAIN IN the car!"
SS guards shouted fiercely, their dogs snapped and snarled on taut leashes. We left our bundles and climbed down onto the platform, which was brightly lit by powerful floodlights. People groaned and cried out as they were hit by rifle butts. Those who fell were hit more and stepped on by others being pushed forward. Panic and chaos were everywhere.

I could see a soft reddish-yellow glow off in the distance. Someone said it was probably a Polish city that the Germans burned.

"Men to the left, women to the right!"

We lined up in rows of five. Aunt Catalina broke into tears as she was ordered away from us. "Joseph! Joseph! Don't leave me!" I heard her cries amid all the shouting and din. I wondered if she'd ever been without him since they married.

Uncle Joseph tried to calm her. "It will be alright, my dear. We will be back together soon. It's just a routine procedure. You'll see. A routine procedure. That's all."

She seemed to calm a bit. "Just take care of Shuly. Take care of him, please." She gave me a kiss on my cheek and hugged me. I was so confused I could say nothing. She caressed my head and told me the separation was only for a while. "Your uncle knows military procedures. We'll be back together soon." She smiled bravely.

Yanosh happened upon us and he hugged his mother and she kissed her son's forehead and promised to see him again. I looked around and saw the same forced separations everywhere. Female SS guards, *Aufseherinnen*, grabbed Aunt Catalina from Yanosh's embrace and dragged her away to a separate group.

We watched helplessly as she was pushed into a group of equally frightened people. My uncle and cousin were sickened, devastated. His promises and vows to protect her could not be kept. The women's group was in the dark but occasional beams of light found their way to them and we saw Catalina standing there, alone in the crowd. One moment she was embracing me, a moment later she was gone into the darkness. It was all so fast. We never saw her again.

Uncle Joseph held me close as we were pushed to the men's group. "Stay with me, Shuly." I had no intention whatsoever of venturing from him that night. Yanosh was looking into the distant crowd. I realized that his family too had been taken from him.

Another floodlight revealed a number of emaciated men in striped work uniforms carrying corpse after corpse from the cattle cars. Their faces were expressionless. There were no such deaths in the car we were on but evidently others were not so fortunate, and people died by the score. The pile of dead grew by the minute, as did my revulsion. The number of corpses soon exceeded those we saw on the sidewalks as we entered the ghetto a few months earlier. The men and boys eventually took notice and gasped. Only few were able to find words.

I knew I would not survive what was in store. This was the end of my short journey. My death was at hand. I once again looked at the soft reddish-yellow glow and the light ash coming down on our hair and shoulders. A revolting stench, quite different from the one in the Oradea ghetto, struck me.

A German addressed us in a stern, intimidating voice.

"You are standing in Auschwitz-Birkenau. You will now go through a brief medical evaluation and after that you will be assigned to barracks. This is a work camp and you are here to work for the Third Reich. For your obedience you will be given warm soup and bread."

Then we were introduced to something that we never saw before and that I experienced again many times – a selection.

A group of doctors and medics in white gowns arrived on the platform and we stood in long lines. I didn't understand what was going on but Uncle Joseph was encouraged by it. "This is a good sign, gentlemen. They need us for work." Yanosh nodded.

It dawned on me that the doctors were assessing our suitability for work. Yanosh was young and strong. Uncle Joseph was older but healthy and strong. I'm sure they worried about me, a lad of fourteen who was healthy but not as tall as most of the males on the platform. I told myself over and over that I was a fine athlete. Still, I looked around and saw most of the around us were taller and stouter.

The night became cool, despite the crowd. Many shivered, though perhaps more out of fear than the elements. I saw the SS gathering old women and children into a large group. The guards and *Aufseherinnen* had pleasing smiles on their faces and often looked into the eyes of women and children and spoke to them to show their benevolence.

"They're sending them to a special area where the young and old are billeted." Uncle Joseph was making sense of the procedures on the Auschwitz platform that night.

"I don't think so," murmured an old man.

He was tall, thin, with a dark beard that I somehow thought needed trimming. He was watching the platform closely too, and drawing his own conclusions.

"I've heard about this. Those poor people have no special billets waiting for them."

Some men looked at him uneasily, thinking he was losing his mind. He would not be the only one. There were wild exclamations and cries here and there; madness was breaking loose on the platform.

"They are going to be killed. I know it!" The man spoke more loudly, his voice quavering, his body trembling. I thought he was ill and about to fall.

"Stop this wild talk this instant! You are scaring the young ones," Uncle Joseph scolded as loudly as he dared. "It can't be! There are women and children in that group!"

The man became quiet.

My eyes fixed on the women and children. Old and sickly men from our lines soon joined them. The SS friendliness continued. I can never forget that. It was as though they were being welcomed to a new school. One guard announced that the men, women, and children in that group would be taken to showers.

As they were led away, people cried out to love ones in other groups. Men wailed like children as they saw their families head away. A few people refused to go. Then more and more did the same. The guards began clubbing them with their rifles. The screaming and crying became louder and more despairing. "No! No! Please no! My family! My family!"

A man broke from our group and ran toward his wife and children, I presume. A guard shot him in the back and he fell hard on the platform only a few yards from his loved ones who screamed helplessly.

I stood frozen and watched as they were led away into the unlit recesses of Auschwitz-Birkenau, where showers awaited them.

A guard spotted an old man among us. He stepped in front of him, almost courteously, and in a friendly manner instructed him to join the other group. We watched as he trod off, I think in resignation. We knew nothing yet of the specific machinery of death there, but we felt death all around us – in the blank expressions, in the increasingly eerie friendliness, in the cold floodlights, and in the soot floating down.

A man right next to me was watching the group led away. He had been on our cattle car – a doctor, we learned on the way. He reached into his coat and removed a small vial. "Goodbye, Sara. We will be together soon." He sent a kiss in her direction and without a moment's hesitation, downed the contents of the vial. I looked at him in horror. People had done it in the ghetto – the old people with Yanosh upstairs. Alexa had tried. He saw the consternation on my face and, softly, even affectionately, whispered, "Good luck to you, young man. Good luck to you." He collapsed and went into convulsions which swiftly came to a stop.

Uncle Joseph, just to my other side, heard me gasp and felt me shudder, and looked at the man lying on the platform, a few twitches were all that was left of his life.

"What happened?"

"I just saw that man drink poison!"

My uncle was horrified as he realized his expectations of a sane, orderly, military-like encampment were wrong – grievously wrong, absurdly wrong. The poor man had been determined to protect his family and for many years had done just that, even through very trying years of the Depression and the ghetto. But it was outside his powers in this place, and he knew it.

The staff continued their cursory inspections, then assigned healthy men and women into work groups. We were marched toward the inside of the camp. We looked around occasionally to make sure friends and loved ones were still close by. We were in a place far worse than the Oradea Mare ghetto. This is where we would live, and this is where most of us would die.

A NEW REALITY

THEY MARCHED US THROUGH THE main gate. I would later learn we were leaving Auschwitz II, or Birkenau, and going into Auschwitz I. There was enough light so that I could make out the words written above it in wrought iron. It read "Arbeit Macht Frei", or "Work Makes You Free." I thought it augured well. Once again, my mind grasped onto hope for fleeting moments.

"Look, Uncle, it *is* a work camp, as you said." He saw the inscription above the gate, too, but events on the platform had shorn him of optimism.

A dozen or more SS guards, with whips and dogs, met us and immediately set upon us. The guards beat us and prodded the dogs to leap and snap at us. We were led to a large brick building illuminated by powerful floodlights. Inside, were guards and prisoners in striped uniforms arrayed at various long tables, each for a particular purpose. I held on to my uncle's hand.

At the first station we were told to undress and place our clothing on wire hangers then place them on one of the many hooks on the wall. Our shoes were to remain on the floor, which was quite cold. A terrible odor hit me.

The second station was for cutting our hair – a task performed by inmates. Our heads were shaved, and to my alarm, all bodily hair was removed. This, we were told, was for hygienic reasons.

My uncle and I moved down to the next where we were given tattoos. "Will it hurt?" I asked my uncle.

"Perhaps a little. But you are a brave lad, Shuly. Besides, I will be right there with you."

My turn came. I had no time to think or try to comprehend. An inmate wiped my left wrist with a less than clean but alcohol-soaked rag then, with needle and inkwell, he inscribed a number on me. I was now a number in a vast system. One number among many.

My number is B14534.[1]

Then I was issued my uniform – a shirt, jacket, pants, and cap. All of them light brown with dark stripes. No socks or underwear. Wooden shoes and a thin blanket. At the end of that station I was issued a small metal bowl. I didn't know then, but soon learned, that my bowl was crucial to survival. Without it, there would be no food given to me. Sickeningly, it was also a portable toilet.

We were shoved out the back of the brisk building into an open area. Not far away reddish-orange flames revealed the dark columns of chimneys and the thick smoke offered to the sky.

A *kapo* – an inmate entrusted by the SS – was assigned to us. He was frail and sickly but nonetheless had authority over us, the

---

[1]   Research later told me that in order to avoid assigning excessively long numbers to the large numbers of Hungarian Jews arriving in 1944, the SS introduced new sequences in mid-May. This series, prefaced by the letter A, began with "1" and ended at "20,000." Once 20,000 was reached, a new series beginning with "B" and so on. Some 15,000 men received "B" series tattoos. I was among the last of them.

precise degree I did not know then. I timidly asked what I think everyone wanted to ask, what was going to happen to us. He initially looked at me sympathetically – a lad hurled into a maelstrom he didn't understand, unlikely to ever know much about life. His face hardened into cynicism. "Do you see the smoke up there? Tomorrow it may be from you." He enjoyed my discomfort.

Uncle Joseph wanted to say something – in objection or in scold – but the kapo went to the other side of the group.

"Don't listen to him, Shuly, he is not telling the truth," my uncle said in reassurance. "We're all going to be working for the Germans. That's what goes on here. Harsh conditions that's all. Hard work and harsh conditions."

I didn't know what to believe.

I looked at Uncle Joseph, Yanosh, and the other men and felt disorientation swirl inside me. Shorn of our hair and wearing identical uniforms, separated from loved ones and terrorized by men and dogs, dehumanized and unnerved, we no longer looked like who we were yesterday, or even like individuals. We were indistinguishable parts of a large, soulless collective. I wanted to wake up. I wanted this place to go away and leave me safe at home in Hungary or Romania.

Instead, SS guards and another kapo marched us to a barracks, or "block," which was back in the Birkenau section. My block, or I should say the one I was assigned to, had been a large stable, perhaps for the Polish army. Rows of rickety wooden bunks which looked like tiers of long shelves went on and on until disappearing into darkness. The odor of mildew struck me on entry. My bunk had a rancid, ragged mattress. I ran my hand across it and felt wet fabric and several straws that poked through rips and holes. There were soon hundreds of us in that block, leaving the air humid and stifling. Each breath promised infection and disease.

"I can't believe this." My uncle whispered in stunned incredulity. "This barracks is filthy. Human beings shouldn't live like this. We have to do something. We have to notify –" His words perished on his lips.

"They'll kill you," Yanosh cautioned.

People lay down, whispering in bewilderment and horror to one another. I settled into my fetid bunk, Uncle Joseph and Yanosh nearby. Uncle Joseph stared at the rafters. As he drifted into sleep, he murmured, "We'll not live through this, we'll not live through this."

———————⌒———————

"Get up! Get up!"

Kapos rousted us from our bunks a few hours later, just as dawn was breaking on the rows of dark blocks. "You have to clean up and be out for roll call in ten minutes. Bunks will be arranged in a military manner or there will be severe punishment for all. *For all!*"

I remained disoriented, partly out of recent events, partly out of the unceremonious wakeup. Uncle Joseph helped out. "Watch me, Shuly. I'll teach you how to arrange things in a military manner. I learned these things long ago. You must learn them now."

I groggily watched him fold his thin blanket in a manner that seemed needlessly complicated. Then we did my bunk the same way and headed for the small latrine that was by then packed with men and boys. Washing up and the other morning routines had to be done very quickly. Kapos, some of them Ukrainians and Poles, mocked us and beat us as we scurried to the field in the cool dawn. We stood in rows and columns, and awaited the first roll call. SS guards paced around us menacingly. Classical music played through public address speakers.

A tall thin man, in crisp SS uniform, stood on a wooden platform as we stood quietly in the assembly yard.

"My name Obersturmführer Koppe. I will direct roll call every morning. I am new at the camp. I arrived only a week ago. However, I was trained by the best. I was assigned this section and I intend to instill strict discipline here."

I stood in the second row and could see him very well. He smiled, exposing bright white teeth. So many smiles from the SS personnel of Auschwitz. He seemed to be an affable fellow. Outside the camp, say, in a town back in Hungary, if I'd come across him, I would not have thought him capable of any cruelty.

"Because you are new here, today and today only, I forgive your tardiness to roll call. Also, I'll allow you to have breakfast in the mess hall *after* roll call. Typically, you will have breakfast *before* roll call."

He paused and looked out at the formation before him, very much pleased by his magnanimity. We relaxed, at least somewhat. So we would not be punished that morning. An icy sternness suddenly took over the Obersturmführer's face.

"But make no mistake. You are here to work for the Third Reich. You are here to work in our factories and other worksites. You will obey camp rules and meet its schedules. Those who do not obey will be severely punished. In order to demonstrate the importance of not being late, I must punish a few of you. Tomorrow morning I expect everyone to be here on time. Kapo, bring five prisoners. The rest of you, *watch and learn!*"

He motioned to a Kapo with a green triangle on his uniform. I didn't know what that signified. I later learned that those with green triangles were criminals – murderers, rapists, and the like – who had become trustees. They were the cruelest of the kapos. Many were crueler than the SS.

The kapo pulled five men from our ranks. I knew something dreadful was about to happen to those poor people.

The Obersturmfuhrer stepped down from the platform and approached the five. Some were uneasy, others terrified. Koppe turned to the assembly once more.

"All of you, *watch and learn!* Anyone late to roll call from now on will be punished like this." Again, a smile. He turned to the five and assumed a superior, official expression.

"You men, lie down! Faces to the ground."

They immediately complied.

He drew his pistol, held it up for all of us to see, and began to shoot into the backs of their heads. One by one, three men convulsed instantly, and died. Blood spurted from their skulls, then slowed and stopped.

A murmur raced through the horrified rows of men. I felt sick.

"No . . . I cannot believe this." Uncle Joseph murmured not far from me. "This isn't happening."

The Obersturmfuhrer's pistol jammed after killing the third man. He tried to clear it and chamber the next round, but could not. The last two men lay before him, trembling, probably praying, awaiting bullets to the backs of their heads. The officer replaced the magazine with the spare in his holster and let the slide fall forward, chambering the round. He killed the fourth man and as he did, the fifth jumped to his feet and started to run. The officer swiftly fired three shots and the man fell to the ground.

"Monster. . . ." I heard people whisper amid the music from the speakers.

Pleased with his marksmanship, the Obersturmfuhrer turned to us. "Now you are to go to the mess hall for breakfast. After that, you'll return for labor assignments. That will be all for now."

"Have your bowl in hand. No bowl, no food," shouted the kapo as we stood in line at the mess hall. There were a few lines. As we understood later, those who did more difficult labor received more nutritional food. As my turn arrived, the kapo gave me approximately ten ounces of brown bread, a dab of margarine, and tasteless, unsweetened black coffee.[2]

"I am not eating this garbage!" One man angrily threw his bread on the floor. Another man picked it up with neither hesitation nor embarrassment.

I didn't know that this would be the only substantial meal for the rest of the day, so I was tempted to eat it all. "Eat only half your bread and drink all the coffee," Uncle Joseph told Yanosh and me. "Save the rest of the bread for later." He was developing an understanding of the place.

"What is done in here violates every international convention," Uncle Joseph said in lowered voice at the table.

"I hear that this is actually a *death* camp," said a man we didn't know. "We are all destined to die after six months. First they'll use us for work, then . . . then they'll kill us all."

---

[2] There was little variation in the meals but we sometimes received a thin slice of sausage or a dollop of jam with our bread.

"My brother is in another section here. He arrived a few months before me," said another man. "They murder people here by the thousands."

"What he said about the smoke was true then?" I stopped eating. "They're burning people here?"

"Yes, they are. First we are worked, then we are killed, then we are burned."

I finished my meal and marched back to the assembly yard with the others.

We were assigned to work groups and under heavy guard, taken to our worksite. On the way, guards and kapos beat us – mainly for personal entertainment, I think. I was hit several times on my back. My uncle tried to intervene and was himself beaten for it. My back hurt badly and I cried. My uncle told me that this was a sign of weakness to them and it would lead to more beatings.

"Show your strength, Shuly. That's the key to survival here. Show your strength."

I stopped crying, though more because I no longer could.

We were ordered to lift heavy rocks from one place and take them to another. I'm not sure it served any purpose, but to wear us down. The sun was hot and we had no water. No rest, no taking it easy. That would mean a beating.

There was a short break for lunch – thin, tasteless soup. Fortunately, I had some of my bread left and that gave me strength.

Most of us survived those first days. As the weeks passed, we lost more and more. Work, malnourishment, beatings, poor sleep. Over and over. I was in a daze but put one foot out in front of the other.

I learned things. I learned that those who arrived at the mess hall earliest got somewhat larger portions – more for breakfast, more to stash away for later. We learned that those who received their ladles of soup late, got a few more bits of the potato and sausage that lurked at the bottom of the pots.

Breakfasts got smaller, sometimes the kapos deliberately spilled some of my soup on the ground, and that of others as well. I needed every crumb and drop, and they knew it. I learned I must not irritate the kapos or SS.

We all became emaciated. Skin became taught against our bones, leaving us with a ghastly appearance. We were being prodded along toward death. Every now and then someone standing for roll call crumpled to the ground and died, or was killed, a few moments later.

There was group punishment for the wrongdoing of one of us. The poor guys arbitrarily selected for collective punishment had to stand all night in the courtyard, shivering, famished, passing out. Uncle Joseph said that, in such conditions, the human spirit has no desire to live anymore. One man said that if he were punished like that, he'd simply sit on the ground and wait for the SS to kill him.

The kapos became crueler every day. Beatings and outright killings were everywhere. A new corpse was an opportunity to get better clothes and shoes. That disgusted me, but only at first.

We had no heat or running water. Hundreds of people used a handful of toilets. Gastro-intestinal diseases were common. Many guys suffered from bouts of diarrhea during the night which made our sleeping quarters even more revolting and hazardous. Every morning we took out people who'd died during the night.

The block was infested with rats and every mattress was laced with squirming insects. Bed bugs were common. They bit me at night and sucked my blood. Lice were constant nuisances. I slept atop my food bowl and shoes, or clutched them as I slept on my side, otherwise they could be stolen. More people were assigned to my barracks and I had to share my bunk with several people. We had to sleep back to back. More than once I woke up to see that one of them had died during the night.

More than once I saw someone with an intense look of despair simply lie down and in a few minutes, gently leave this world. Some people grabbed hold of the electric fences around the camp in order to put a swift end to it. I think they reasoned it was better to go out on their own terms than on those of the Reich.

Auschwitz was designed to kill us. We would perform hard labor for a while, but there was no mistaking where we would end up. Almost every day we went through the selection process in which we were judged fit or unfit for labor. The latter were either shot then and there, or led away to one of the gas chambers at the north end of Birkenau.

After six weeks or so, Yanosh and I thought Uncle Joseph was weakening by the day. We offered him some of our bread but of course he refused. The three of us sat outside our block and enjoyed the little quiet and privacy available to us. It was late spring, the skies clear. The stars flickered above us, innocent of any knowledge of what went on under them.

Uncle Joseph assessed the situation. "We are not working for the Third Reich. We are being worked *to death* by the Third Reich. It is calculated, planned – here or back in Berlin somewhere. There is method here. We need to do something."

There was conviction in his voice, not mere lamentation.

"What can we do?" I asked.

"We need to make a plan to escape. Otherwise, we'll all die, sooner or later. There's no other way out." He looked at Yanosh. "You boys are strong and can survive longer than most, but even the young and strong cannot live long here. Look what's happening around us. Every day people fall to the ground."

"And we have to carry them back to the block," Yanosh added while looking downward.

"We live like rats in old basement walls," Uncle Joseph continued.

"The rats have better chances," Yanosh noted wryly.

The idea of escape was appealing but no one knew how. All I could think about most nights was rest and tomorrow's breakfast. I found my bunk in the dark and climbed up. Sleep came easily at times.

One day we were assigned to sort the belongings of a group of newly arrived inmates – things they had to surrender on the platform, things that had belonged to people who were now inmates or dead. This sorting area was called *Kanada*, as it was deemed a place of wealth and opportunity. It was light duty. Occasionally, workers at *Kanada* found items of food in the piles of baggage.

I was given a pair of scissors and instructed to cut open the linings of clothing and luggage, especially expensive looking ones, and search for hidden valuables. I once found a few photographs. There was a family of four – mother, father, and two daughters. They posed in a tree-lined park, the joy of being together clear on their faces. I wondered if any of them were still alive.

Another time I was assigned to one of the special work details, or what were called, *Sonderkommandos*. These details worked at the gas chambers and crematories and, regretfully, I saw them in operation. There was an anteroom in the gas chamber building, which itself was an ordinary-looking brick building. A group of people were led to the building where they were to undress and take showers. There was a sign in the anteroom in German – a language most Central Europeans had some knowledge of:

> Put shoes into the cubbyholes and tie them together so you will not lose them. After the showers you will receive hot coffee.

The people were pushed into the chamber itself, a dank concrete room with only ventilators above. Small children were thrown in through a small aperture. I recall an SS guard took a few infants by their tiny legs and smashed their skulls against the wall.

Gas canisters dropped from men on the roof. Immense generators atop the building started up and ran on high. The tremendous roar they put out was to drown out the screams of the victims below.

I was too close to the building. I heard the screams of the victims. Men, women, and children. Horrible sounds, unforgettable sounds. I especially recall hearing the children. The children should be in school or playing in parks back in Hungary. Instead, they were being gassed to death in a shabby room in southern Poland. On and on came the sickening screams. At length, perhaps fifteen minutes, they stopped.

After the ventilators cleared the toxic gas from the chamber, we entered. The SS fired their pistols into the heads of anyone showing signs of life. Remaining rings and other items were taken. Hair was cut and placed in sacks that were transported to factories. We arranged the corpses in piles of ten, then took them to the ovens.

One day, while still on the *Sonderkommando*, there was an event that neared the miraculous. A girl of about ten was being led along with many other women and girls to the gas chamber. They were coming straight from the platform and hadn't had the time to learn of the camp's nature. I was outside the building awaiting the aftermath, which I knew, and which she did not. A line of hapless people awaited their final education. It was her fair complexion and blonde hair that I noticed. There was no one close to her. She was alone.

Our eyes met. I looked into the eyes of a poor girl who had no idea what was ahead. I all but fell into her blue eyes. On she walked.

I found myself raising my hand and waving to her, as though we were in a schoolyard or park. She waved back, but instead of feeling joy and hope, I was overpowered by sadness and hopelessness. I cast my eyes downward, ashamed of my tears and my secret.

Then I thought that she was all alone and that she needed me. It was selfish not to look at her. I needed to give her a moment of human connection as she continued her walk. However brief that moment was, I owed her that.

Our eyes met once more. She was sad but then suddenly cheered. Tears fell down my cheeks and I made no effort to hide them. It was a moment of complete vulnerability and honesty.

She was puzzled why I was crying. Then she understood. I'd told her. My tears and moment of withdrawal had revealed everything. I forced a smile on my face, but she walked on.

The SS shoved the women and girls into the anteroom, but there was confusion and scuffling, and the process stalled. The girl grabbed hold of the doorway. A guard pushed her ahead but she held on. His rifle butt crashed down on her head and back. Blood came from a gash on her face. I found myself running to her, an idea only beginning to form.

I grabbed the guard's arm and shouted, "You must come outside and see what's going on! You're needed!"

He recognized me as a boy in the *Sonderkommando* and in a sense, part of the operation.

"What is it?"

"Something just over there!" I struggled to come up with something amid the screams and confusion of the anteroom. It came to me. "A prisoner! She's trying to escape!"

He mulled over his conflicting duties and after a moment, let go of the girl. As the SS guard came with me, I glanced back and saw the girl wipe blood from her face and run past the other busy guards and away from the building. I didn't know where she went, perhaps to the women's blocks where they'd try to protect her.

"Where is this prisoner? Where?" The guard glared at me angrily.

"She was right there! I don't know where he went!"

My head exploded into a thousand dazzling stars as his machine pistol came down hard across my forehead. Down I went. His boots pounded into my sides and head. His presence needed back inside, he left me bleeding on the ground. I came to my feet and returned to my work detail. I was in tremendous pain, blood trickled from my roaring ear.[3]

---

[3] A year later, when I returned to Oradea, a friend told me a story of a similar incident at a gas chamber. The girl was able to escape to a block in the women's camp. She went through the Death March from Auschwitz and was liberated at Bergen-Belsen. I cannot say it was the same girl I saw but I feel something wondrous took place that day.

Not long thereafter, I helped remove another heap of corpses from the chamber. Knowing I'd helped one girl live another day. I felt a small moment of victory.

———————

The days on the *Sonderkommando*, despite my small victory, left a void in my being. The cruelty of fellow human beings and the piles of corpses, horror and agony frozen on the faces of adults and children and babies, made it clear to me that there was no greater being watching over us, and we were not part of the unfolding of that being's intricate plan. I never wanted to hear another utterance of religion again.

ADOLF EICHMANN COMES TO AUSCHWITZ

I GOT TO KNOW SOME OF the many people in our block. People came and went, but I got to know a few of them, if only for a short while. Our conversations were usually brief. Some were quite memorable. I got to know Eliezer, or Eli, chiefly because of a bold plan he concocted.

Eli was older, perhaps in his forties. There was an exceptional alertness in his eyes. His grey hair was limited to the sides and at times it looked like small wings had cropped up there. It amused me but as a boy I held my council on the matter.

A teacher before all this, he'd absorbed all the information he could to add into lectures and discussions. Now, he was ever watchful, not simply for guards and kapos – we all did that. He kept his eye on every detail, in the block and on worksites. And he listened.

Eli was assigned to the officers mess, where junior and senior officers ate, socialized, and told stories. Eli went about his duties, his ears ever listening. He knew which generals were respected and which ones had been sacked. He heard about how the war was going and he knew there would soon be two fronts as the Americans and British and others were expected to land in France soon.

Naturally, I'd heard the name Hitler back in Oradea. Everyone had. But it was from Eli that I heard the names Göring, Goebbels, Keitel, Himmler, and the rest, including Adolf Eichmann.

He heard about the SS hierarchy and probably came to know as much about it as most of the officers dining around him. He knew who was liked, who was disliked, who was up for promotion, and who was going off to a frontline unit. He knew about the systematic nature of the camps. There were work schedules, production schedules, and even train schedules for gathering up Jews across Europe and bringing them to Poland.

The officers chatted away, oblivious to the presence of a deferent inmate who entertained them with old jokes and confessions of ignorance. They laughed at him and saw him as an amusing, idiotic Jew, and even gave him scraps to eat as signs of their munificence. But Eli was taking their every utterance down in his constantly turning mind.

In the evenings Eli gave reports. Most were uninterested. What difference did his observations make? Would they help in morning roll call or out at a worksite? Most slipped off to their bunks to get every bit of rest they could. Uncle Joseph and I listened. It was a diversion, it was entertainment. We didn't have the BBC, we had Eli.

He was upset by the passivity of the inmates. There should be more resistance, more fighting back. We were lambs to the slaughter. His bold talk did not fit well with his humor or with reality for that matter. Uncle Joseph thought Eli was off his rocker – *meshuganeh*. I'd seen many of those. But Eli held my interest.

"Did you know that Adolf Hitler himself has never visited any camp?" He asked us one night. "Did you know that?"

Of course, we didn't. How would we know? We didn't listen in on SS table talk.

"Not once. His underlings have, though. They come to make sure everything is proceeding according to plan, especially in light of recent events in the war."

I wasn't sure if he was displaying his wit or leading up to something. "The officers at the mess discuss Hitler's notable absence. They speak to friends at other camps, so they know. They think their *führer* is simply too busy to come to one of the camps. But it's perfectly obvious why Hitler stays away!"

Judging by the blank expressions before him, he had to enlighten us as to the obvious.

"Hitler knows what's going on here and knows what's in store for those who administer the camp system. Hitler wants no evidence that he knew of this place and those like it."

It sounded right to me.

"What if he *doesn't* know about what's going on here?" someone asked.

"Ha! That cannot be. He knows what goes on in his Reich but he doesn't want any evidence to point to him. He's deluding himself, though. He's in charge, he'll be taken to book. No doubt about it."

My uncle voiced strenuous support for Eli's position. Eli nodded in appreciation.

"I learned something very important this day, my friends. We shall have a very important visitor in a few weeks. Herr Adolf Eichmann is coming to pay us a visit."

"Who is Adolf Eichmann?" I wasn't the only one unfamiliar with the name.

"This Eichmann fellow is an important figure in the Nazi death system." Eli relished his attention. "I heard much about the man and I also asked many in the mess hall about him. He directs the train system that brings us here. And one more thing. Did you know that Eichmann is an expert in Judaism?"

"Why would a Nazi have an interest in Judaism?" came an incredulous voice.

"Oh yes, oh yes. Eichmann studied our religion, history, and customs. He even learned Hebrew. That is why he was given the task to solve the Jewish problem for the Reich. He rounds us up, packs us into trains, then brings us to Auschwitz or one of the other death camps. Yes, he's one of the major figures in this."

Eli paused with a proud look on his face that signaled another piece of news was coming.

"And Eichmann is coming for an inspection in May. I will soon learn exactly when."

"Why do you want to know that?" someone asked.

"I intend to assassinate him," Eli said quietly.

"What?"

"How?"

"I've formed a plan. I can't let the opportunity slip away."

Eli's announcement elicited looks of admiration and skepticism, sometimes on the same faces in a matter of moments.

"My friends, I'll be the one who'll kill Eichmann. I just need help with a distraction."

Eli outlined his plan. Eichmann was scheduled to observe a morning roll call and Eli would set upon him with a knife he'd take from the mess hall where he worked during roll calls. He wanted some of us to cause a commotion that would distract Eichmann's bodyguard just before he set upon him. When it was objected that anyone who'd caused the distraction would be killed, Eli insisted that once Eichmann lay dying, all attention would be on Eichmann and his assassin.

"Perhaps, perhaps," Uncle Joseph said. "But perhaps not. The guards will recognize the connection and eventually punish those who caused the distraction. Nonetheless, I like the idea of fighting back like soldiers!"

My uncle wanted to fight back, so despite his skepticism, he listened.

"This is a risk we have to take to fight back. I am willing to die in this endeavor. It may save the lives of others. I'll know the exact date of Eichmann's arrival shortly."

That night in the bunks, I asked my uncle what he thought of the plan.

"I really don't know, Herman. Too many things can go wrong. There's too much left to chance. But I do like Eli's spirit. Yes, I do like his spirit. Just not his plan." He shook his head and exhaled.

If my uncle had doubts, I had them, too.

—◦—

The next evening Eli brought pen and paper that he'd taken from the officer's mess. He drew a map of the roll call yard, the stand where Eichmann would be, and where he, Eli, would be upon leaving the mess hall – with a knife.

"I'll stab him repeatedly and then I'll die. I accept this."

My uncle suggested searching for a more intricate plan but Eli was adamant. Eichmann was coming and he had to be killed this way. There was no alternative.

A handful of men announced that they were in. They would cause the commotion and Eli would do the rest. Eli thanked them.

Nothing changed in Uncle Joseph's mind.

—◦—

A few nights later, Eli brought word.

"He'll be there in three days!"

He looked to his fellow conspirators, and their eagerness indicated they were still in. The group went over the plan again and again.

The night before Eichmann's arrival, Uncle Joseph and I met with the group. We weren't to participate but Uncle Joseph wanted to express his respect for the men and wish them the best.

"Tomorrow we'll make ourselves felt, and we'll bring change," Eli said serenely. "It was a great pleasure knowing you gentlemen."

We all shook hands and retired to our bunks.[4]

—◦—

That morning Uncle Joseph and I were sent off to work well before roll call was finished. I looked back as we marched away but saw no

---

[4] According to Yad Vashem, Eichmann came to Auschwitz several times in the spring and summer of 1944.

commotion or important visitor. All day we labored eager to get back to the block and learn how Eli's bold plan unfolded. That evening, after the mess hall, we looked about for one or more of the initiates but couldn't see any of them and were reluctant to be seen making inquiries.

At last we came upon a man who had met with Eli and the others but who had not promised to be part of the diversion. When he saw us, and our interest, his crestfallen appearance told us all but the details.

"It was sad. I stood near the front and could see a notable visitor surrounded by bodyguards and more officers than usual. They all looked crisper than usual and those closer to Eichmann fawned over him. I looked for Eli and soon spotted him walking toward Eichmann. There were so many guards around him!

"I waited for the distraction; men were supposed to argue and fight. I waited and waited. Eli kept on toward Eichmann. Still no distraction. I looked around and saw the men who were to cause the commotion. They stood there! They just stood there!

"Eli was getting closer. I saw no knife. Maybe he was determined to kill him with his bare hands. He had a look of cold determination. When Eli got within twenty meters of Eichmann, an officer drew his pistol and shot him down. Four or five bullets hit Eli and he fell to the ground.

"Eichmann showed no interest. One officer said, "A stupid Jew! That's all he was." The others laughed. I don't think they even suspected what Eli was trying to do. He probably shot him simply because he was out of place. Maybe he killed Eli to impress Eichmann. That was it. That's all that became of Eli's plan. A good man, a brave man."

There was less interest in what happened that morning than I would have thought. Uncle Joseph praised Eli as a courageous man and went on to say Eli had insufficient knowledge of military matters to devise a sound plan.

"He certainly had the spirit of a soldier," I said.

"Yes, he did. Unfortunately, no one will know what happened this day," Uncle Joseph noted ruefully.

That night I thought how much I wanted to set eyes on this Adolf Eichmann. I wanted to see if he was as evil as Eli said. I thought he must look monstrous, more so than the guards and kapos who terrorized us.

After the war I saw photographs of him, and years later I saw him put on trial in Israel. I watched the proceedings on television, as did most of the nation. He didn't look evil, though he was. It was a case of the "banality of evil" that observers speak of. Banal, but evil.

I also later learned of several attempts to kill Hitler. Why did men like Eichmann and Hitler survive attempts to kill them? No, there was no higher design at work. It could not have been part of a divine plan. I didn't believe in such things anymore. Somehow, however, I hope that when Eichmann was hanged to death, word reached Eli.

THE RED CROSS VISIT (JUNE 1944)

NOT LONG AFTER ARRIVAL, SELECTION, and processing, everyone in my block, and a few other blocks, were taken to another section of Auschwitz-Birkenau. The Auschwitz complex was many square kilometers and no inmate knew all its complexities, only the ones we worked in and the darker ones we learned indirectly of. We lined up and an officer addressed us.

"You are now assigned to this section and will stay here one day. It is a privilege to be here. You'll be sleeping in better barracks and eating better food. You'll be issued new clothes and shoes and bowls. You will work in a nearby section where you'll assemble parts for our military. You will remain in one group and listen to new supervisors. Obey them! Any disobedience will be severely punished."

The prospect of generosity from the SS, even if admittedly temporary, naturally gave rise to wariness among us. I thought of the Germans who gave me chocolate in Oradea.

"I don't like this. I hope this doesn't mean it's our last meal," said another man bitterly.

With that sobering thought, we entered the new block.

We were amazed, though still wary of course. Clean and spacious. Soft mattresses, fresh bedding and even pillows. The air was odor-free. Auschwitz with amenities, one might say. Guys hopped on mattresses, claiming them for their own.

Uncle Joseph and Yanosh were behind me. My uncle remained on guard. "This is fishy. They're up to something."

The three of us sat down on mattresses near one another. We ran our hands over the clean soft fabric. Yanosh lay down and stretched his arms and legs.

"Don't get too comfortable," Uncle Joseph cautioned. "This isn't how it appears. It's a ruse of some sort. A shameful ruse. I don't understand the nature of it yet. But this will not last long."

We all wanted to know what the game was.

"Everyone outside to the roll call yard! Now!"

We lined up and were marched to a nearby mess hall. I marveled at how clean it was, inside and out. Long tables covered with cloths. Pitchers of coffee and water on every one of them.

An *Aufseherin* asked, almost politely, for volunteers to help serve breakfast. I was puzzled by her gentleness. Requesting volunteers was not the way things were done. She asked once more and a few became servers for that meal. The rest of us sat and shortly later, breakfast was served. Dark bread and eggs. The water and coffee pitchers were refilled periodically.

There was little conversation. In part because we were so suspicious, in part because we were busy devouring the food.

The *Aufseherin* spoke once more.

"Now you'll be issued new uniforms."

An hour later and we had fresh clothing and new shoes. Then we were taken to a workshop where for several hours we assembled metal containers with military stampings on them, Wehrmacht or Waffen SS. Warm potato soup and bread arrived for lunch. The servings were generous and seconds were given.

We assembled in the yard that evening, and the same officer spoke.

"Tomorrow, we will have visitors from the Red Cross. For those who don't know, the Third Reich is a signatory to the Geneva Convention."

"So that's the game," my uncle whispered.

"They will bring you packages. You will receive them in the dining hall. You are forbidden to talk with the Red Cross people! Those who do not obey this order will be severely punished. The packages are yours to keep. Now you can walk about the yard until ten pm. Dismissed."

It was a strange feeling to walk about freely for a few hours. Yes, of course there were a dozen SS guards watching us, but we took what we could.

"So the guards are putting on a show for the Red Cross," Uncle Joseph said as we walked about. "And we have small parts in the show."

"But not speaking parts," Yanosh added.

"Right, son. We'll be back to the old arrangements shortly after the Red Cross cars leave the gate."

"At least we can enjoy decent food and bunks," I added in boyish naivety. I accepted the arrangements as fraudulent and short-term, but I saw them as a most welcome break – a vacation of sorts.

"It's a trick of the worst kind, Herman. Don't get used to it. It will be gone before you know it. I'm thinking of speaking with the Red Cross personnel. We need to get word out."

"They'll *kill* you!" Yanosh warned.

"If I can get the message out, it will be worth it. It's my duty."

He was right, or at least might have been. Nonetheless, I didn't want to see him shot down on the spot.

"I'll try to talk with them tomorrow," he said in the bunks that night.

In the morning, as we assembled for roll call, cars with Red Cross insignia were nearby. A few men with the same insignia conferred with SS officers. The conversions seemed casual. I heard occasional laughter.

Uncle Joseph was angry.

"The ruse is playing out before our very eyes. Those bastards are tricking the Red Cross into thinking this is the real Auschwitz. I know the Geneva Convention. The Germans have to allow the Red Cross to inspect so they built this facade and placed us here for a short time."

I feared for what might happen to us after the inspection.

SS guards began unloading packages and taking them to the mess hall. The ranking SS officer continued to chat amiably with the delegation, then he pointed to us. We were led to the dining hall where the *Aufseherin* had prepared our parts in the show.

"After breakfast, each of you will be given packages from the Red Cross. You'll take it to your block and leave it there. You'll be able to open it upon returning from your work. Now, eat. You have a full day of work in front of you."

Breakfast was served, dutifully if superficially observed by the delegation and their SS tour guide. As a nice touch, we were given apples. I partook of more than one and suffered from stomach aches later at the plant. We were given our parcels, each marked with the Red Cross insignia, and taken to the block, all under the eyes of the delegation.

My uncle seethed. He wanted an opportunity to speak with a Red Cross official, but none presented itself. The SS maintained a distance between the delegation and us. The same was true as the delegation looked at our workplace. Judging by their faces, they were satisfied with what they were seeing.

That evening, we stood in the yard as the delegation inspected our block. Shortly thereafter, they climbed back into their vehicles and drove away.

Back in the block I opened my parcel and was pleased to find a chocolate bar, tea bags, tins of meat, pudding, biscuits, cheese, and condensed milk. There was even a small bar of soap. The inspection was a fraud, but I enjoyed the gifts from Switzerland.

"I suggest that you hide as much of these items as you can," Uncle Joseph said.

I ate a few things and hid others.

An hour later guards entered the block, shouting at us and kicking the boxes about.

"Leave everything here and get outside, now."

After roll call we were led back to our regular blocks. Blows fell hard and often along the way. One came down on my face, sending me to the ground where I was repeatedly kicked. Bleeding profusely from the mouth, I stumbled into the block and found my bunk.

The Red Cross inspection of Auschwitz had concluded.

ALONE

F ALL CAME TO SOUTHERN POLAND and morning roll calls and selections took higher tolls. Colds and respiratory infections were increasingly common and we took corpses out every morning.

Work assignments involved building new buildings in and around the main camps of Auschwitz and Auschwitz-Birkenau. Think of Auschwitz as a small town with surrounding villages that were all engaged in the German war effort and its Final Solution. The two overlapped: we contributed to the war effort and in so doing we were worked to death.

We were ordinary workers – low in the Reich's labor hierarchy. Workers at Monowitz, a chemical plant, and Bobrek, a factory making parts for planes and submarines, had better blocks and more nutritious food. They were skilled workers and more valuable. We were unskilled and utterly expendable. New trains of unskilled laborers pulled into the station routinely. We heard the locomotive whistles and the clanging of cattle cars as they came to a halt. Sometimes we saw the bewildered and terrified faces.

Uncle Joseph was in decline. He was malnourished, he'd been beaten and humiliated, he'd been worked to exhaustion day after day, and he'd lost his wife. It was the absence of his beloved Catalina that hurt him most. He tried to look strong for Yanosh and me, but his efforts were less and less convincing. He was coughing more and more.

Every night we talked outside before the block was shuttered tight.

"My Catalina is gone. I know it." He murmured somberly one night. "I know it."

"There is no way to know that with certainty. She may be at one of the sub-camps." Yanosh held on to measure of hope for his mother – and for his own family as well. We'd all asked other inmates we came across at work sites. It was part of prisoner life to learn what they could about friends, family members, and how the war was going. Everyone was in the same plight and everyone shared what information they had. Still, we'd seen Aunt Catalina and Yanosh's family assigned to the weak group when we arrived on the platform that night.

"No, I know that she could never survive here. Even if she started as a worker, she could never endure it. I know it. I can feel that she is gone, I can feel it. A husband knows."

We remained silent. He was probably right. She relied on him to give her strength. Too much so. She had a very hard time of it in the Oradea ghetto, and here, without him? If Yanosh thought his wife and children had shared the same fate, he kept it private. I think he knew, though.

"There is no way to be certain." My words were half-hearted and I'm sure they sounded that way. At some point, optimism was childish.

"Yanosh, I want you to watch over Shuly. I promised his parents." I saw despair and tears in my uncle's eyes.

"You're still here to watch over me, Uncle Joseph. We all help each other."

He hugged me. "Yes, of course I'll be here with you, Shuly. It will not be for long, though."

Yanosh offered more words of encouragement. He struggled to hold in his own emotions. He clasped his father's hand. "You can hold on. We'll help you at work, we'll share our food."

Uncle Joseph coughed lengthily, his throat making a disconcerting rasping sound. I'd heard it before in other guys. It almost never cleared up, though it always stopped.

"I'll do my best, boys, but a man knows when his time is at hand."

It was too hard to show strength and confidence that night.

"Look, this is the way of the world. There's no need to be sad. I've been blessed to live with you, my big boys, for many years. I've enjoyed watching you become fine men. I love you both. I've been truly blessed."

A look of calm came to him.

"And you'll still watch us grow." My words might have been a little stronger.

"Of course, of course. But just in case, I want you two to remain together. Yanosh, you are to watch Shuly. Stay with him. Make sure no one takes his belongings, and help him on details. You two have to see each other through this."

He coughed noisily into a dirty cloth he stuffed into his trousers. I saw flecks of blood.

"Yanosh, do you promise me?"

"Yes, of course, we'll stay together – always."

"Shuly, you have to promise me that you'll be strong. You'll keep your strong spirit. You and Yanosh are young and strong. You must survive. It will be our victory."

I did promise, though I was feeling weaker by the day.

The next day we continued construction work around the plants operated by IG Farben, a large German chemical firm that made artificial rubber.[5] The site was in the Monowitz camp, which was also

---

[5]   One of its subsidiaries, I learned after the war, made Zyklon B – the gas used in Birkenau's gas chambers.

known as Auschwitz III, and was located about five kilometers west of Birkenau.

A group of SS officers and civilian engineers arrived to inspect the work site. Later we were told that one of them was SS head Heinrich Himmler, though I cannot be sure this is true. At the sergeant's command, we stopped working and lowered our heads as the officials drove past.

As the men inspected the site, an old man in our group fell to the ground and called for water. The SS guard who oversaw our detail, a stout, red-faced sergeant, approached the man. We knew the sergeant enjoyed his power over us and indeed enjoyed killing one or more of us as he saw fit. He aimed his rifle at the man and put a bullet through his head.

The officials looked over but showed no great interest. They continued with their inspection, occasionally looking at blueprints, pointing at particular places, and conferring on matters. It looked like the inspection was going well.

I was peering into another world. There in the entourage were engineers and surveyors. They weren't SS or Wehrmacht or Nazi party officials. They were what I might have thought to be ordinary civilians. They wore ordinary clothing. They had ordinary faces, not the famished or cruel ones I knew. I thought they might be horrified by a summary execution. They conferred once more and, satisfied, they left.

I watched and learned.

One or two more men died of exhaustion that day. We carried their corpses to a large pit just outside the Birkenau fences where piles of dead accumulated, from worksites or the morning dead from the blocks. When there were enough bodies, a mass immolation ensued.

The next day was the coldest yet in the fall of 1944. We shivered badly during morning roll call and on the trek to Monowitz. I worked hard, not because of a sense of duty, of course, but because to ward off the cold. A man laugh not far from me.

"Little man, you make me laugh!"

I knew the voice – it was that especially brutish sergeant's. I turned to see him looking at me, his malevolence plain.

"Go on. Keep working, little man. I can use a little entertainment this day."

What was I doing? Working too hard to stay warm? I gradually slowed down to a normal rate.

"No! No! Faster! I enjoy seeing a little man work so enthusiastically. We need more like you!"

I resumed the previous pace, all the time thinking how much he liked to torment victims before beating them – or killing them.

Suddenly a powerful blow come down on my back, sending me to the ground. I cried out, but only for a moment. Worse I feared was coming, and in a way, it did.

"Leave him alone!" An unfamiliar voice challenged the sergeant – unwisely, I thought. A man in his thirties stood in front of the sergeant, shovel in hand and ire in his sunken eyes. Though we were on the same kommando, it was the first time I heard him speak. "You can't treat us like animals!"

I lay on the ground and watched a familiar scene play out. Some men saw death coming sooner or later and opted to accept it now, on their terms, with at least a measure of dignity. Some grabbed hold of the electric fence, some stood up to guards. The result was the same.

The sergeant wasn't angry. He said nothing. He simply drew his P-38 pistol and fired three times into the man. "Yes, I can," he noted calmly. In his estimation, a rule was violated and he handled the matter promptly and professionally.

I was afraid he'd shoot me too, as I'd begun the incident, at least as someone like him would reckon things. I returned immediately to work, hoping his bloodlust had been sated for the day.

I felt his presence right behind me. I heard him light a match and smelled cigarette smoke.

"I didn't forget you, boy."

This was it. He was going to kill me. I turned slowly and saw his face. I was relieved that his pistol was holstered for the moment.

"Leave the boy alone!"

I knew that voice. It was my uncle's. He looked to me and nodded. Yanosh was a little farther away, anxiety etched on his face. Uncle Joseph's eyes forbade me to do anything. "Stay still, and live," he seemed to say. He dashed toward the sergeant like a soldier in the heat of battle. The sergeant began to draw his pistol but my uncle was upon him and seized it from his hands.

"You are in violation of international treaties. You are not soldiers, you are murderers. *I* am a soldier and I will die like one."

Uncle Joseph fired and the guard looked down awkwardly at the hole in his tunic. Smoke then blood came from the wound. Another shot, and he fell to the ground, mortally wounded if not dead. Kapos called out for more SS but they were well on their way already, rifles and machine pistols at the ready.

"There is one less monster at Auschwitz," he announced. Pistol down at his side, he was strangely calm, and content. "I am weary. You and Yanosh must go on. I shall be with Catalina." A few shots slammed into him. He crumpled to the ground, and many more hit him.

"Back to work! All of you, back to work!" the soldier shouted, brandishing their weapons. We complied.

I cannot speak for all the men on the kommando that day. Most are probably dead, if not from the SS then from the many intervening years. But in addition to my grief, I was proud of my Uncle Joseph.

As dusk came to Monowitz, Yanosh and I carried him back to the block in Birkenau. We gently placed him where we had less gently placed so many others who were unknown to us, but loved by others somewhere in Europe. We might have cried, or we might have been too tired and confused.

"He was very ill, coughing blood more and more. He was a fine soldier in the previous war – honored and revered. He died a soldier this day."

Yes, he'd been an honorable soldier, that day and before. And a good father and guardian. He saved my life that afternoon. He gave up his own for mine. I said I wanted to die that way too, killing a brutish guard, then accepting my fate like a man. But Yanosh reminded me that we promised to do everything we could to survive. My promise had to take precedence over my indifference to living and my will to take vengeance.

"We must live through this," Yanosh whispered almost prayerfully amid the pile of dead.

I nodded.

We couldn't do anything more. We gave Uncle Joseph a last hug and went back to our block. In a few hours, a kommando would take the dead to the pit outside the fences where they'd be set alight in a few days.

The young man I shared my bunk with looked at me. He was used to see me arriving with my uncle. My desolation told him all.

I woke up and realized once again that I'd lost my uncle and guardian. No more help in the morning, no more assurances, no more guidance. I could hear him say the war would be over soon and we'd be back in Oradea not long thereafter.

Yanosh and I continued the practice of talking outside at night about family and home and normal life. We even made plans about what we'd do after the war, after Auschwitz. Uncle Joseph was with us still.

A week later, at morning roll call, our block was divided into three groups. One group was to go to Monowitz to work in the Farben chemical plants. The second was designated for Neustadt and Bobrek. The third was to remain in Birkenau for general labor.

Yanosh was sent to Monowitz.

I remained at Birkenau, alone.

ESCAPE

ALONE AND DISPIRITED, I BECAME ill and weaker by the day. I passed out a lot and was quickly helped up by fellow prisoners, whether on labor kommando or at roll call.

Mornings were colder, roll calls more arduous. More of us died every morning. One morning, I stood in the assembly yard along with several hundred others, awaiting orders. It was cold, the rain soaked my uniform, and wind gusts increased the misery. The wait was longer than usual. Most of the SS were elsewhere, probably indoors, and the kapos were running the roll call – rather incompetently by camp standards, I might add.

The man in front of me fell to the ground and didn't move. He might have died standing up. I'd seen it. Over the next half hour, several more of us passed out or died. My teeth chattered and my skeleton-like body shook. My body was numb and I felt weaker by the moment. I struggled not to fall as so many around me already had.

We were low-priority labor. Another train would bring more any day, maybe later that day.

The kapo calling roll stepped into the faltering rows and columns and came to me, a lone boy standing, if barely, among many prisoners lying on the ground or struggling to get up. He stood right in front of me and grinned, his stained, gnarled teeth inches from my face.

"Aren't you the lucky one? One of the last left still standing in your row."

His eyes conveyed power and disdain. I wondered why. After months in the ghetto and camp, I had seen much hatred but never grasped its cause. I did him no harm and neither had anyone there that morning. Useless to ask, then or now, but that's what was going through my mind.

He marked my name on the roster and then, without any warning, hit me on the face so hard that I fell to the ground, my nose bleeding profusely. As I tried to stand, he kicked me repeatedly in the face and ribs. I fell back down and lay there. No more kicks came, no pistol shot sounded. He thought I was dead, like the others around me. I had had enough and was ready to die.

I knew what was in store. I'd be collected with the dead or near-dead and taken to the incineration pit. It had its attractions that morning. A dozen plans raced through my mind, and they all hinged on getting dumped into that pit for the dead.

The pain got to me, and in its way, it helped me. I passed out or assumed I was dead and lay back in acceptance of whatever afterlife was in store for a youth already cast into an abyss.

Consciousness returned later. I looked up at a dark sky, then around me. I was in a heap of foul, stiff corpses. The stillness and settings were unearthly. I was dead or near to it, and my present thoughts were akin to the twitching of a man in his last moments. In time, however, it was clear that I was alive. I had been hauled to the pit.

I knew the kapos and SS would be gone by now, nonetheless I stayed where I was and stared at the stars in the inky sky. I looked around furtively, saw no one about, and decided to take my leave. I was startled to see another body move, and he was equally startled to see me. We stared at each other – two boys, barely in our teens, too scared or too smart to make any sound at all.

We looked about in the moonlight and saw the fence and a guard tower. We knew that was south. To the north we saw woods and without any words, we began to make for it. Strength and youth returned to me, if only barely. I thought at times I could have run back to Hungary that night, though I fell occasionally and had to rest every half hour or so.

We didn't know each other's names, but we were a team. We crossed the field, stumbling only occasionally in our wooden shoes, and ran toward the stout trees of the forest. We'd been taught in our childhoods that forests were dangerous places where careless children get lost or devoured by wolves or bitten by venomous snakes. The forest that night was shelter, rescue, deliverance. Nothing could be as dangerous as what lay behind the fence we were running from. The scent of pine was a wondrous departure from the vile stenches of rotting corpses, fetid blocks, and chimney smoke.

My companion, almost as out of breath as I, signaled to halt. We sat on a fallen tree and caught our breath.

"I am Herman."

"I am Shmuli."

We shook hands then listened hard, familiarizing ourselves with the sounds of rustling branches and night creatures so that we might better recognize a sign of danger, such as a German patrol.

"How old are you, Herman?"

"I am fourteen years old, and you?"

"Sixteen."

"Did you arrive with your family?" I asked hesitantly, even though it was a common question inside the camp.

"Parents, two sisters – Yuliana and Anatolia. And you?"

"Uncle and cousin."

No one wanted to ask the obvious. It was Shmuli that broke the silence.

"None of my family is still alive. I know it."

"My uncle died not long ago. I don't really know how long ago it was. My aunt was sent straight to her death at the platform. My cousin was sent to Monowitz."

"There's some good news at least. Monowitz workers are deemed valuable. They are treated better than those in the main camp, like us."

I nodded in agreement and held out hope for Yanosh. I didn't know what to say about his loss. Sorry was terribly insufficient and it had become trivial over the last few months. Everyone had losses. A simple nod sufficed. It conveyed more than you'd think.

"My uncle insisted that I find a way to survive. He said people like me had to let people know what was going in here – in *there*, I mean." I pointed behind us.

"He's right. We have to let people know. Someone will come to help."

"Do you think the Germans will come after us?" I asked.

"We were corpses, not workers. They won't notice two missing corpses. So many of them back there."

"Good. We need to get far away from here, though."

"I heard guards talk about partisans in the woods. We have to find them. But we need to be careful. There might be patrols – Germans and villagers in their pay."

Shmuli was knowledgeable and that comforted me. I was tired and hungry. He read my mind.

"Let's try to sleep here until dawn. Then we'll look for food and clothes. These inmate rags will give us away in a moment."

We slept in close proximity, as we did in the blocks. I lay awake for an hour with one thought – I was away from Auschwitz.

I woke up in a panic. I was late for roll call and. . . . The morning grays above the pines greeted me, not the dark rafters of a block. I had to piece together where I was and how I got there. I felt I had won a small victory.

It was cold, though only autumn. Shmuli was balled into a fetal position. I waited for him to wake up. He soon did.

"How long have you been up?" he asked groggily.

"Ten minutes."

"Let's get going."

"Yes. let's go."

We walked deeper into the forest and came across berries of some sort or another which clung to their twigs and lay on the ground. There were risks in eating them but they looked more appetizing than the leaves and twigs. We ate a handful each. No more.

We came across a rippling creek, a little frost along its banks, and drank from it. Clean water. We headed upstream where we found deep, still water. Two foul-smelling boys hopped into the cold water and became cleaner than they'd been since they were packed into cattle cars in summer.

"Where are we going?" I asked. Judging by the sun, it was late morning.

"Well, we have to find partisans. They'll help us and we'll join them." Shmuli spoke with brave noble purpose. "The Germans killed my family. I want to get back at them."

"They killed my aunt and uncle."

"And your parents?"

My parents. . . . My parents had become distant memories, as was everything before arriving at the platform.

"They're in Romania, in a town called Focsani. I don't know what's become of them. Maybe they're in a ghetto. Maybe they're somewhere in Auschwitz."

"I heard people on my kommando say that the Germans haven't done nearly as much in Romania as they have elsewhere. They'd ask about people from Bucharest and no one knew of any."

"Maybe there are camps in Romania and everywhere else."

"That could be, Herman. But if so, that's why we must become partisans."

So we were to become soldiers. Off we marched, in search of partisan bands. Finding none that day, we covered ourselves with leaves and branches and went to sleep.

We awoke to odd clanging sounds in the distance. We stealthily walked a hundred meters toward the sound and peered into a clearing – a meadow, with cows, a few wearing bells around their thick necks. The peacefulness and beauty of that scene transfixed me.

Seeing no one about, we decided to treat ourselves to milk – a basic part of youth denied us for many long months. We were unable to find a bucket, so Shmuli demonstrated the fine art of drinking directly from the udder. I thought it dangerous. Even a city boy like me knew that cows were prone to kicking, perhaps all the more so if someone besides a calf should go for a drink down there. I watched warily as he put his mouth near the udders and tugged away until milk squirted out.

Hunger overcame worry and I lay under the cow. Shmuli and the cow did the rest. It was the best nourishment I'd had since arriving in Poland some months ago.

A man's voice interrupted our repast. He was probably speaking Polish. We turned around in panic.

It was an old farmer – stout of build and non-threatening in demeanor. He could still inform on us and reap a reward, or at least avoid a harsh punishment. We were ready to make a break for the trees at any moment.

Then he spoke in German, more or less the lingua franca of Central Europe.

"You boys certainly know cows. I am Emil. And who are you two?"

"I am Shmuli and this is Herman."

"You boys look like you've had some hard days. Are you hungry?"

We nodded silently.

"Come, it is breakfast time. I am up since four o'clock this morning."

We followed him a half kilometer to a cabin surrounded by a few chickens and goats. Chimney smoke augured safety for a change.

We sat in chairs before a well set table as Emil fried potatoes and eggs for us, which he then served with bread and goat cheese. He sat at the head of the table and watched us eat. He told us he lived alone. His wife had died five years earlier and his son, devastated, died not long after that.

"Where did you escape from?" He noticed our anxious looks. "Don't worry, I'll not hand you to the Germans. We Poles have hated them for centuries."

"Auschwitz," Shmuli replied.

He became upset. "Those bastard Nazis put kids like you in a work camp? You are children! You should be in school!"

Shmuli and I looked at each other. He spoke first.

"Auschwitz isn't a work camp. It's a *death* camp."

"The Germans murder people there. Thousands and thousands," I added. "They send trains filled with people from cities across Europe and then they work them to death or kill them with poison gas."

Emil looked skeptical. "Who told you these stories? I'm hardly one to defend Germans but even they would not do such things."

We recounted our experiences at the platform, in the selection yard, on work details. We described the blocks and our food. We told of the deaths of loves ones and guys next to us. He looked at our gaunt faces and eyes deprived of youth, and the truth set in. He'd probably heard much the same from villagers closer to the camp, but refused to believe them.

Saddened, even sickened, Emil sat wordlessly – an elderly man learning from boys that the world was darker than he'd dare believe.

"You two stay here with me. The war won't last much longer. The Russians have entered Poland. They'll be here before long. I doubt they'll be gentle with those Germans. Stay here."

Naturally, we agreed. He gave us work clothes and a clean place to sleep. There were occasional patrols in the village and rural roads, and if a patrol were to near Emil's cabin, we were to make for the woods until they left.

Mornings we would rise at dawn. No shouting, no beatings, no selection. Work on the farm was easy. Shmuli and I returned Emil's kindness and courage with a good day's work. We became healthier and stronger. The world was a decent place again.

FARM WORK AND MUSIC

W E WOKE UP EARLY EVERY morning. We milked the cows, washed them, and tended to the pigs. The hogs were immense, at least to a city boy. Emil told us that hogs were highly intelligent animals and though I was naturally skeptical, I soon saw unmistakable signs of intelligence, cleverness, and even humor. I enjoyed taking care of Emil's hogs even more than I did the gendarmes' horses.

Emil said he would hide us until the war ended, and after that he'd enroll us in a school in Ostrava. Shmuli and I had found an uncle. For now, however, we had to be careful. He took us to the cellar and pushed an empty barrel aside. There was a cool draft. He explained that this was a tunnel that led to just outside the fence from which we could make a run for the woods, should it come to that.

Our Polish uncle cared for us, for our help on the farm, out of sympathy for two lost boys, and out of loneliness. One day he brought Shmuli a watch from the village market. "Swiss made," Emil noted with pride. It was wartime and people had to sell miscellaneous things to get by. Most memorably, he one day brought me a violin. I was overwhelmed by memories of my aunt and uncle in Oradea and my living room concerts.

Emil's face betrayed expectation. A glance to Shmuli indicated the same. So I played. Probably not well, but my audience was appreciative all the same. Student pieces came back to me. Dinner from then on was followed by a recital for my family. Afterwards I thought back to my home, and wept.

Emil returned from the market one afternoon in an especially buoyant mood. There had been a young girl there that day, about my age, who played guitar and sang, much to the enjoyment of the people young and old. A few coins were tossed her way. Emil suggested I play with her and bring home a few coins, too. I objected, though not strenuously, and the following week, I was off to the village market, violin in hand.

Stands selling all sorts of things were set up at one end of the village commons. Being almost winter, there was little in the way of fresh food but people brought jars of fruits and vegetables and cheeses wrapped in cloths to sell or trade. Women knitted articles of clothing and offered to darn worn clothing. It was a scene filled with more life than anything I'd seen since entering the ghetto.

I heard the sound of chords from a well-tuned guitar and the mellifluous voice of a young girl. A few steps and I saw her. She was sitting on an upside down bucket, guitar on her knee. So lovely. Blonde of hair, attired in a dress likely reserved for Sundays and other special days like that one. A pink cloth was spread out before her and people occasionally tossed in a small coin.

I stood wordlessly.

"You see? She plays very well."

Shmuli saw my eyes and said, "It is not simply the music that has reached his heart."

It was true. It was plain to all. She caught my gaze and to my delight, she smiled. She smiled to me! Then her lips moved and through my daze I was able to realize that she'd asked my name. Her voice was as lovely in spoken word as it was in song. She needed to repeat the simple question to this awkward lad. I told her my name.

"My name is Emily. I see you have a violin. Do you play?"

"Yes, of course he plays," Emil answered for me. "Herman, play for your new friend."

I somehow managed to nod and she asked me to stand next to her. A dozen or so villagers gathered around. I placed violin to chin, making sure my left wrist remained covered. "Go ahead," she urged.

Properly encouraged, I began – first with a simple student piece, then into a more challenging work. All from memory. My ability to read music was probably gone by then. Determined though I was to hold in my emotions, memories of youth coursed through me. I concluded the melody a bar or two early and dabbed my eye before a tear could fall. Our audience there in the marketplace applauded and I again had to preempt a tear or two.

"You play so well, Herman! Please, let's play together for a while!"

I shyly agreed. Emil said he'd be looking around the stalls and to enjoy myself.

Emily and I played. At first we'd alternate but soon enough she followed along with a melody I'd play. Her chords, my melody. An hour later, the pink cloth had a dozen or so coins from grateful villagers. It was a princely sum to the two young performers.

We took a break and she offered me bread and cheese that her mother had made. My blissful morning was broken when she asked where I was from. I was prepared to run for the cellar, sprint to the woods, but not for a simple question from a pretty girl. I told her we were from a village near the border with Czechoslovakia. I wondered if my accent betrayed that I was from much farther south than that.

"And where do you come from, Emily?"

"I live in Václavovice. We had a farm but after my father died a few years ago, my mother and I raise chickens on a smaller place. It's lovely, though. Mother's a few stalls away, selling a few chickens if she can. My father gave me my guitar when I was a child. I make a little money as you can see. Together, mother and I get by. It's hard because of the war, but we get by."

It didn't matter what she said. I was enchanted by her voice. Yes, the same could be said of her eyes and hair and everything about her. It seems not every ounce of youth had been taken from me. I probably blathered a few things, careful not to reveal too much about how I came to be in southern Poland.

The time raced past us. Emil returned to pick me up. To my delight she asked if I could visit her and her mother in Václavovice the following Saturday. I was elated when Emil nodded.

On the way home, Shmuli asked how old she was and if I liked her. I replied she was fifteen and she meant a lot to me already. He and Emil cautioned me about what I might tell her.

Saturday arrived, at last, and we made the hour-long trek by horse cart to Václavovice and Emily's home. We had a light meal – not many people in Europe had large meal in those days – then we played music. After a short concert, Emily and I walked outside on the farm, her mother along with us, of course.

"So, where did you say you live?"

"Oh, I am originally from Oradea but we moved to a village in Poland."

"What's the village name?" her mother asked.

"Ah, it is near a town called Oświęcim."

"Is it as lovely as our village?" her mother again asked.

"Václavovice is much lovelier."

Her mother continued to ask questions about my family and my uncle's occupation. I answered them obligingly, though not in great detail.

"Herman, let's take a walk." Emily took my hand and we walked toward the forest where a brook wound its way to a creek then to a river. She invited me to sample it and I knelt and did just that. Cold, clear, rich in minerals. I thought back to the brownish water I had to drink a few weeks ago.

"What are you hiding, Herman?"

The question startled me.

"I just know you're hiding something. I can see it in your eyes. They look away at times."

I was frozen. I wondered if I should make a run for it.

"Your mouth lies but your eyes tell the truth. Is it your family? Was your family not kind to you? Is that why you and your brother moved here?"

"No, my family was very kind to me. My uncle gave up so much for me."

She held my hand and warmth spread through me. I felt trust and honesty.

"Shmuli and I escaped from a Nazi camp called Auschwitz." I spoke quietly and looked straight into her eyes.

"Auschwitz? Where is that? I don't know it."

"It's German for Oświęcim. That's all I know. It's a death camp."

"*Death* camp?"

"Yes, a camp for killing Jews."

"Jews. . . ." She spoke the word in shock, or something close to it. "So you are Jews then." She nodded silently. "The Germans came to our village and told us about them. They are taking Jews from all the towns and villages."

"Yes, and they do so in order to kill them at Auschwitz."

I told her of the Oradea Mare ghetto, the cattle car journey, and in general terms, what happened at Auschwitz. I spoke honestly as though getting word out would help.

"I am so sorry, Herman. I didn't know. I always saw the Nazis as stupid. Now I understand that they are evil. Why doesn't anyone do anything?"

"Please keep this our secret. No one can know. If the Germans find out, they will kill Shmuli, Emil, and me."

She gave me her word.

Toward evening Emil and I headed back. Since that day, Emily and I met once or twice, to sing and talk. She was the first girl I fell in love with, but I never told her that. I think she knew it, though. A love-struck boy gazed into her eyes and held her hand and told the truth. Yes, she knew it.

One day at the marketplace, as Emily and I played to a small gathering, two German soldiers walked down the rows of stalls. I made sure my cuff covered my tattoo. They continued to come closer until they stood before us, enjoying the youthful musicians. Emily launched into another melody swiftly. The Germans seemed to be enjoying the show. Then one of them spoke – to me.

"You are new here. Where did you come from?"

"I arrived only recently to live with my uncle."

"What's your name, boy?"

"Herman."

"Your last name?"

As planned, I gave them Emil's last name – Babic.

"And where do you live, Herman?"

"Near Ostrava."

"And where is your uncle?"

"Right there." I pointed to Emil and Shmuli, hoping my hand wasn't trembling much.

"How is the music business today, my boy?" Mercifully, Emil came over to help out. Shmuli was with him. We looked at each other cautiously.

"You, are these your children?"

"Alas, no. They are my wonderful nephews from Lublin, where my sister lives. They are here because it is safer. Wonderful boys, no?"

The Germans seemed satisfied and sauntered away.

On the way home, Emil decided it was best that we not go to the marketplace anymore. There'd be other Germans who'd ask questions and might not be as easy to put off as the pair that day. Seeing my disappointment, Emil promised to take me to Emily's in a week or two.

That night I played my violin more yearningly than ever. Emil thought that I was eager to make up for losing my marketplace rehearsals. That wasn't it. I played because I was scared and music calmed me.

Saturday with Emily . . . it still sounds so pleasant. We talked of growing up in Poland and Hungary, in a small village and in a large city. Sometimes I spoke of Auschwitz, mostly I didn't. I preferred to talk about Anton and the gendarme stables. Better for young hearts to talk of more pleasant things.

One day, as we walked not far from her home, Emily kissed me – on the lips. It was unexpected, it was baffling, it was wonderful. I had no idea how to respond. She was amused by my startled response. I think I blushed.

"Are you embarrassed?"

"No. . . ." I must confess I wasn't telling the truth just then.

She gave me another kiss and I was able to simply enjoy it. We stood there, two young lovers.

"It will be over soon," Emily said. "My mother says that the war will be over soon. You won't have to hide anymore."

As we walked back toward her house, there were two horses tied out front. We sensed danger.

Emily directed me to hide in a silage bin. I climbed in and kept as still as possible. After a few minutes I heard the voices of German men. Soldiers. Possibly the ones in the marketplace. I peered out between slats and saw them leaving. They thanked Emily's mother, mounted up, and rode off slowly down the dirt road.

Her mother explained that the Germans were asking about the boy her daughter was playing with in the market that day. They were still suspicious and had likely reported their suspicions to superiors. That's what the German garrisons did – watch for anything out of the ordinary. Emily admitted that her mother knew about me but quickly insisted there was no danger. Her mother's reassuring look convinced me.

"I don't think you should come here anymore, Herman," her mother explained to me. "The Germans are suspicious and they will ask more people around here about you."

It was clear that my Saturdays with Emily had come to an end. We hugged each other more closely than we'd dared before.

As Emil and I rode off, I looked back one last time. I waved goodbye to my first love.

From then on, Shmuli and I stayed around Emil's cabin, our eyes ever on the watch for a German patrol and mindful of the shortest distance to the cellar or woods. Every evening we packed a little food in the event we had to make a break for it.

We helped out on the patch of land but even that had risks. Emil told us over and over that the war would be over soon, as the Russians had crossed the Polish border to the east. We listened for the thunder of artillery and the buzz of aircraft, but if we heard anything it was likely our imaginations and hopes getting the best of us.

A sense of dread nonetheless befell Shmuli and me, and we talked in resignation that our dread would, though some unknown agency, bring great harm down on us. All three of us.

Over the months Shmuli and I learned of Catholicism from Emil, and he of Judaism from us. Emil even made braided bread for Friday meals – a Shabbat in a Nazi-occupied land, complete with candles. In addition to our hero and savior, Emil was becoming a father.

One evening we heard cars roaring down the dirt road – more swiftly than we'd heard other motor vehicles come by. Emil, clearly concerned, peered through the window.

"Black cars! Gestapo! Down to the cellar! Now!"

My dread was becoming event. I felt sick to my stomach. Shmuli and I ran to the door but I looked back.

Emil looked at me in great distress. "Go! You have to go now!"

We rushed to him and embraced him. We looked into each other's eyes and I saw he recognized his hour had come.

"I'll always be with you. You are my sons and I'm proud of you. One day all this will go away. I love you both very much. Now go!"

He all but pushed us out the back. We scurried to the cellar opening and clambered down into the dark, mindful of where the tunnel was. Above us, we could hear knocks at the door then voices.

A man introduced himself as a German officer, less gruffly than might be expected. In fact, he was disarmingly polite. He asked about two young visitors and Emil said he had two nephews from Lublin with him, but they were away just then. That sounded bad to me. The officer said that he checked with his sister in Lublin and she had no children. When Emil protested that he must have spoken to the wrong person, the officer curtly said there was no mistake, then added that hiding Jews was a grievous offense.

Shmuli and I inched toward the tunnel, bags of clothing and food in our hands.

The officer told Emil he was in serious trouble and that they would find the Jews. To our dismay, Emil began to berate the Germans for killing innocent people. He shouted to their faces about ghettos and cattle cars and the death camp not far away. The Gestapo agents ordered him to shut up but he went on about gas chambers and smoke.

Two loud gunshots sounded.

Shmuli crawled into the tunnel with me right behind him. We made our way as fast as we could to the opening near the fence. After Shmuli peaked out and saw it was clear, we crawled out. I looked back and saw Germans looking through the barn and sty. I paid a moment's homage to our friend and father, then ran for the protection of the Polish forest.

We walked along trails through the woods for hours, headed for Emily's village where I thought we might get information or a little help. We crawled into foliage and waited for dawn.

I could see the village and along its edge, Emily's house. I was fearful of bringing harm to her yet I desperately wanted to see her again, if only from a distance. Young hearts, foolish hearts.

Her house was still. Chickens ran about the yard, pecking about for seeds in the cold ground. No sign of Emily or her mother. A little closer I saw the door was ajar. How could I not investigate? I stealthily made for the back door and looked into the kitchen. More of my dread had played out into event. Emily's mother was sprawled awkwardly on the floor, numerous bullet wounds plain. Just past her, the body of my Emily, in the same pitiful state.

I felt rage inside me. If I had a machine gun I would have taken on the German army. Then sorrow and nausea reduced me to a sobbing boy.

I wrote a short note and left it on the table. "I love you, Emily."

We walked for days, searching for the much rumored partisans. I was beginning to think the rumors were only that. There were villages here and there but we dared not go in them. Exhausted and increasingly incoherent, we fell asleep. We were soon awakened by the sounds of footsteps and voices – Germans. Shmuli got up and ran for it but was cut down by submachine-gun fire. I lay there in fear.

I was taken into a holding station where I was beaten and asked for information on partisans. I had nothing to tell them because there was nothing to tell. I was taken to a train station and packed into a cattle car of the Death Express. I collapsed and fell asleep.

The following day, I looked out the cattle car slats and judged we were heading west. Hours later, a familiar routine played out with me in it. We were herded out of the cars and made to stand in formations. Despite my reckoning of heading west, I was sure I was back in Auschwitz.

Then I heard an SS officer announce, "You are now in Dachau."

DACHAU

"YOU ARE NOW IN DACHAU."
The words and inflections were familiar, though of course not in a comforting way. I looked out and saw other familiar things – confused and worried faces, signs of hope from those who thought a work camp was better than a ghetto, men in one line, women and children in another, distraught faces and agonized separations.

I was too weak to think clearly and I'm glad for it. Otherwise, I'd have fallen into profound despair and the slow spiral downward. I solemnly went through the procedure. No one seemed to care that my left wrist had already been tattooed. I saw two or three other people going through the process with similar markings.

I was herded into a block with my blanket, shoes, and metal bowl. It was even more crowded than the one at Birkenau. Two, sometimes three people shared the same bunk. The stench of feces and urine was everywhere. I was used to such things back in the Polish camp, but after my weeks with Emil I thought they were all behind me.

I walked down the dark aisle searching for a place to lie down. There were either too many people already or gruff refusals from bigger guys. I was near the back when I heard a boy's voice.

"There's room here."

I saw a boy's head. Dark hair and filthy face but kind eyes and a trace of a pleasant demeanor.

"Thank you." I murmured as I climbed up on the bunk. The straw mattress was moist and smelly.

"Sorry. I peed in my sleep two nights ago. My name is Leon Hirsh."

I liked him immediately.

"My name is Herman Rittman. Don't worry about the mattress. I am used to such things from Auschwitz. Actually this one is in fairly good shape compared to what was back there."

"You were in Auschwitz?" Astonishment was in his hushed voice. Other people heard and turned to look at me.

"Unfortunately, yes."

"And how did you end up here?"

"Well, that's a long story, Leon."

"We're not going anywhere! But first let me tell you of your present camp."

His wit amused me.

He arrived from Munich and was alone. His father had already been sent east by train. His mother was taken with a group of other women to work in a sub-camp of Dachau. He had spirit still. Wit and spirit. I benefited from both.

Leon explained that Dachau was a labor camp and he knew of no systematic extermination program, the outlines of which I'd mentioned and which he and others had heard of.

The conditions, I came to learn, were about the same as at Auschwitz. Long roll calls in bad weather. Deaths from infection and malnutrition. And SS guards beat people to death or simply shot them with a round from a pistol or rifle.

Dachau held political prisoners, criminals, homosexuals, and minorities that believed in other religions. We stayed away from the criminals as they were their own caste with they own ways.

Leon and I worked on the same kommando, mostly in a munitions factory. I polished artillery shells. Other times we worked at the Messerschmitt factory where we made aircraft parts. This was not the most arduous work at Dachau. Others worked outside at hard labor. I had moved up in the system. Every two weeks there was a selection process and those who failed, were sent east, to Auschwitz.

Leon and I became friends. But I must confess that neither one of us became too close. That was the case with most friendships there, especially after many months. There was always the knowledge that the friendship could end very suddenly and very violently, and the emotional cost would be devastating, perhaps catastrophic. Everyone knew it.

Leon kept hidden away a booklet with his father's poems and thoughts – a diary of sorts. One of the last entries was:

I am leaving on a train
I don't know when
There's no need to pack
From this train there's no way back.

One night, before lights out, we heard shouting and gunfire and cries not far from our block. We lay down in our bunks, hoping it would pass. More shouting then countless staccato bursts of automatic weapons.

"There will be bodies to deal with in the morning," someone down the aisle whispered. He turned over with a long sigh and went back to sleep.

A boy of seven snuck into our block, terror on his young face.

Leon motioned for the boy to come with us. His face had been hit hard, by something more than fists. Rifle butts perhaps.

"Climb up with us, boy."

He eagerly complied.

"But stay quiet."

The violence continued nearby, then at lights out, everything fell silent.

"What's your name?" we asked in quiet whispers.

"Andrei" he replied. The little light that came in showed the face of a boy in shock. "They killed my family – parents, brother, and sister. I don't know what happened. I just ran. I couldn't stop running in the dark until I reached this place."

"You are a brave boy, Andrei," Leon said. "You can stay with us. We'll take you to work tomorrow."

"We are all orphans here," I said.

He lay down and cried with his fellow orphans.

In the morning we had to think quickly about a plan for Andrei. But what? We couldn't just take him out to roll call then off to the factory. He was too small. The only thing to do was hide him in the block and bring him a portion of our meals.

We were pleased to see him return to life – talk, laugh, and play. He'd find a piece of wood and it would become a car he'd push around the floor while making motor sounds. We brought him some of our meals but somedays there wasn't any because a kapo would punish Leon and me for a transgression or just because he wanted to. Andrei was disappointed but he accepted it. He'd even pretend he was eating, much to our amusement.

He became our kid brother. It was a strange feeling to have someone depending on us for his life.

We wanted to smuggle him out of the camp. He wasn't on anyone's roster; he wouldn't come up as missing in morning formation. We looked for gaps in the fence or holes underneath it. The camps were rarely as solidly laid out as thought. We knew that from the Oradea ghetto and even Auschwitz. Look as we did, we found nothing.

In the evenings, before lights out, Andrei would stand with us outside. It was safe, or reasonably so. We'd stoop to minimize the height difference. No kapo or guard would see anything amiss. It was just a handful of prisoners talking among themselves before being locked in for the night.

Andrei would ask us, "Why? Why has this come upon us?"

We were older and I suppose this made him think we'd thought the matter out and arrived at an answer. Everyone in that camp, Auschwitz, and all the other camps, had asked the same question, probably every night as they looked to the skies – the same skies that people in faraway lands looked up at in wonder, ignorant that people faced dreadful deaths beneath the same skies.

We never had an answer. Not for Andrei or anyone else. His loved ones had been murdered before his eyes. There was nothing to be added.

Others in our block accepted Andrei's presence, risky though it was. They even brought him morsels of food from the mess hall, as did Leon and I. We were all in the same plight. Andrei's youthfulness appealed to us. Ours were gone.

Winter was coming. Southern Germany is no warmer than southern Poland as best as I can tell. We kept each other warm as we slept, but alone during the day, Andrei was terribly cold and in a few days, became ill. Fever, chills. Both worsened. We applied a cold cloth to his forehead. It didn't help. He was losing weight and interest as well.

Yanek, a doctor in our block, took a look at him, as he did for all the infirm in our block and adjacent ones. He had only his experienced hand to gauge Andrei's temperature, and his reading was not welcome news. About 40 degrees Celsius. "Everyday we see this here. Everyday." Yanek walked away.

I thought of a way to cool Andrei off. Leon and I helped him outside and we placed him in a few inches of snow, then scooped up more for his head and torso. A few minutes of this and we helped him back in and warmed him up. The shivering was down and so was his temperature.

Andrei and I spoke for a while. He spoke remorsefully of being unfair to siblings. I said I was sure they were small incidents and they all knew how much he loved them. When he asked me if I thought his family members were in heaven, I had to pause.

"I'm sure they are, Andrei."

He looked to me and smiled. "It's good to have an older brother, Herman."

I woke up and saw the light of the new day. Andrei's fever was back, maybe worse. Furthermore, he was unresponsive. Yanek came over and gave another brief look. He shook his head. "Brain damage, possibly. I've seen it here many times. Too many times. Very sad, very sad. Perhaps it's for the best."

One by one, pale emaciated men walked by. Some looking on sympathetically but only briefly. Most just walked by. Leon and I were nearing despair.

An older man approached us. Long gray beard, educated, more life in his eyes than the rest.

"I'm Rabbi Mendy. Is the boy your brother?"

"His family is all dead. But I am his brother all the same."

"I understand."

"Can you help him?"

"No, I cannot. But someone greater than us can. Let us say a prayer for. . . ."

"Andrei."

"Let us pray for Andrei this morning."

The three of us joined hands and the Rabbi began to pray in a strong voice – this in a block where people whispered fearfully. Then Rabbi Mendy touched Andrei's forehead and offered a silent prayer.

"It is not in our hands." He quietly left.

Leon and I hid Andrei and went off for breakfast and roll call.

My mind stayed with Andrei as I worked at the parts factory. After trudging back to the barracks area, I immediately went to check in on Andrei. I looked but couldn't find him. I feared the worst. A kapo? A guard? Did someone inform on us? Then I saw his face groggily appear from beneath a dirty blanket.

He was feeling better and his appetite had returned. We happily gave him bread and a little dab of jam that we were given that evening.

The doctor came by and gave Andrei a look. "No fever as best as I can tell. Well, a miracle here in Dachau." He shook his head and left. "A miracle . . . but for what."

I looked at the cheerless parade of emaciated men. The skin of the faces was taut across their skulls, making them look half-dead. On and on they came. A few showed a glimmer of joy and hope in their eyes as they looked at Andrei, the miracle boy of the block. The doctor saw the glimmers too and I saw the same thing come across his face. "Maybe there's hope. Maybe some of us will see this thing through."

I didn't re-find religion that night. There were subsequent events that would undermine anyone's faith. But I was amazed. I had *some* hope. I hoped I'd be able to help Andrei survive Dachau.

———

There was a guard named Fritsch. He was memorable for his cruelty, standing out among the ranks of SS guards at Dachau. Beatings and killings were part of his daily work. One day, as we marched in the cold, he called us to a halt. He walked through our columns as we shivered. His face was red from the elements, his eyes flared as he contemplated what was to come.

"You, step out!" He was clearly speaking to me. I complied quickly. "You, step out." He shouted to another man.

On it went until fifteen of us were taken out of the group. I'd seen this before. He was going to shoot us. To my surprise I became calm, more suddenly and completely than I thought possible. A quick death from a bullet was more agreeable than more months of this, after which I'd die one way or another anyway. I had the calm of someone who knew death was at hand and accepted it. It was an amazing moment.

My sole concern was Andrei. Who would take care of him? Leon I knew to be on the downward spiral.

Fritsch pointed to a wooden rail that was left from an old gate that had given way long ago.

"You!" He pointed at me. "Step forward and stand under the slat." It was difficult to take a step.

"Step forward and stand under the slat, I say!" he bellowed.

Slowly I walked to the bar. My head barely touched it.

"Just as I thought." He came so close I could smell his breath. "What is your name?"

"Herman."

"Herman, it is a lucky day for you. You have set the height standard for this day. Others will not be so fortunate. Anyone taller or shorter than this slat does not belong here." He looked at me to see if I comprehended. I did.

"Herman here is going to live. All you others, form a line. Hurry!"

A boy reached the bar, and his head didn't reach the standard. Fritsch shot him in the head and he crumpled to the ground.

The next man was taller than the bar. Fritsch shot him also.

The next was taller. So was the following man. Only three of us lived through it.

Back in the block, I hugged Andrei and told him I almost lost him that day. He asked for no elaboration. He simply held me.

That night, after lights out, we spoke.

"Herman, do you think that right now there are children somewhere in the world who have happy lives? Their parents put them to sleep, read them a bedtime story, and they just fall asleep without any worries of someone killing them in the morning?"

"Of course, Andrei, in many places in the world it's like that. And one day it will be like that for us. All this will end and we'll be back to normal lives."

I'm not sure how convincing I sounded. I thought back to my uncle.

"No, Herman, life will never be the same for us. We've lost our families. We'll be given away to someone. And after all that we've seen here . . . we're never going to be children again."

"We'll survive this and you'll come with me."

"Thank you, Herman. But I don't think I'll live long enough to see that day."

"Stop it, Andrei. You're young and strong. You will make it. We both will."

"I hope so."

Where was this world of happy, safe children in loving families? Where were these people?

The following day, on the march to the factory, an SS guard pulled a prisoner from the formation and beat him with a club. Another prisoner suddenly shouted to leave the poor man alone. The guard summoned his comrades and they formed a circle around the two inmates and beat them unconscious. We were all punished by standing in the cold for an hour.

We had musicians, artists, teachers and doctors among us. One musician had a violin and played for us sometimes. I really don't know how he got a violin but nobody cared. We enjoyed his music immensely. I wanted to ask him if I could play but it would have made me think of Emily and Oradea.

One morning two guards entered the block.

"Wake up, all of you! Wake up!"

We jumped from our beds. I covered little Andrei with my blanket and told him to lie still.

They walked down the barracks.

"We have reason to believe that you are hiding a young boy. One or more of you are keeping this child."

They relished the fear they saw.

"Before we perform a thorough inspection, we'll give you the chance to disclose the child's whereabouts. If you surrender him now, there will be no harm to any of you. I promise you. We are fair men."

A painful moment of silence followed.

"Bah! We don't have time to go through this. We have schedules to meet. If you do not surrender the child to us now, we'll have no choice but to begin executions, starting with *you*."

A guard grabbed a man who cried out and covered his head with his arms.

The guards enjoyed our fear. When I think about this now, I think we should have rushed them, seized their weapons, and shot them. Yes, we would have been killed but at least we would have had a moment of revenge or justice. Instead, we stood by.

A guard aimed his machine pistol at the cowering inmate on the floor and fired a burst into him. The poor man's body convulsed as each bullet hit, then fell still. Other inmates groaned and screamed until they were ordered to shut up.

"Where is the boy?"

Silence.

Another prisoner was thrown to the ground and shot to death.

"We will kill everyone here unless we get what we came for."

How did they find out, I wondered. How will this end?

The guards went into a frenzy of beatings. Rifle butts flew, men screamed, blood was everywhere.

A voiced called out from the din, "Stop!" and strangely, the guards did just that. I looked over to the bunk but Andrei was gone. Then I knew whose voice it was.

Andrei walked toward the SS.

"Stop beating these people! Stop killing them! Here I am. I am who you're looking for!"

He approached one of the younger guards, no more than twenty.

"I had a family not long ago. You killed them! I am alone now."

The guards looked around at the mayhem, then at this young voice of reason. The young guard was unnerved. The other saw discipline slipping away. He raised his machine pistol at Andrei and let loose with a dozen rounds. Some hit the floor and the walls, but a few hit the poor boy. He slumped to the floor clutching his stomach and chest.

"You killed me . . . goodbye."

Satisfied that their mission was concluded, and more than a little stunned, the SS left the block.

I held Andrei and thought about the happy children somewhere in the world, far from Dachau.

"Come, Herman, let us say the Kadish for Andrei. He is in good hands now."

It was the Rabbi. We cleaned Andrei's face and arranged his tunic. The weak smile I thought I saw as he spoke his last words was there.

We said the Kadish. A few joined us. Then we carried the small body out and gently placed it among the bodies of other people who'd died in the night.

Having lost the younger brother I wanted so much to protect, I became listless and inattentive. I was urged on by fellow inmates, especially the Rabbi, but I too wanted to say goodbye. My weight declined to about thirty-five kilograms.

Typhus struck, taking away dozens of us a week. A few were from my block alone. Camp administration issued masks to the guards. Any inmate who got too close to a guard was considered trying to infect him, and was shot down. We carried corpses to roll call each morning so that they too could be counted. The Reich kept its books up to date.

There were many non-Jews with us at Dachau. There was a young gentile named Kurt Traven, who was a political prisoner. I saw him beaten by guards at roll call and later noticed that he worked at the artillery shell plant where I was. I saw him milling about a nearby block one evening and approached him. After introductions, we spoke.

"I see you at the plant. You are German, aren't you?" He nodded. "Why are you here?"

"I belonged to the White Rose." He spoke proudly, a rarity. I think being reminded of his past enlivened him. "Do you know of it?"

I shook my head. What would a flower have to do with being sent to Dachau?

"They were young people, mostly students, who tried to build a movement against National Socialism. We were in Munich, not far from here. I am so sorry for you and your fellow Jewish people. I am ashamed of what my country is doing, here and elsewhere. I hope there is justice someday."

Schools were a frail echo in my mind. Somewhere there were young people who went to classrooms and listened to teachers and prepared for their futures.

"What did you study in school?"

"Journalism. We need to tell people what goes on in the world, in their own country. Germany is such a beautiful country with a rich culture and wonderful traditions. It's all being destroyed."

"You are thoughtful – and brave."

"Well, look where it brought me." He laughed cynically. "The leadership should be assassinated and only then will this end. Maybe someday. But how along have you been here?"

"A few weeks. I was in Auschwitz before. I escaped but then caught. I was sent here."

"Is it true what they say about Auschwitz?"

I told him of the selections and gas chambers.

His mind reeled. What he knew of Nazism barbarity was important and righteous, yet it was almost trivial compared to what anyone at Auschwitz knew. The cruel ideology he'd seen in Munich had constructed grinding machinery to the east.

"These people will stand trial one day."

Kurt was confident of this. I didn't believe in justice prevailing in the end.

"What kind of punishment will they get? A little boy was just shot to death by an SS guard. What kind of punishment will his killer get?

I saw SS guards smash the heads of small babies and gas thousands of people. What kind of punishment fits?"

"We are a great nation, we have morals!" His voice was elevated, but he wasn't angry. It was more that he felt terror because of what his people were doing and he feared what would happen to them when the war was over.

"Kurt, I am sure many good Germans tried to stop this. Some are here, others may be dead."

"Oh yes. This I know for sure. The Gestapo caught me and brought me here along with many others. Others were put to death. I expect other people to have more courage. I want to do more. Ahhh, I have to go to my block before lights out." He looked at me closely. "These sons of bitches will have to pay for what they've done. I want both of us to see it."

It was time to get back inside for lights out. I said goodbye.

———⌒———

Not long afterward, I saw Kurt argue with an SS guard at the munitions plant. He accused the soldier of crimes, murders, and disgracing Germany. The guard was outraged. He shouted that political prisoners were worse than Jews. He was on the verge of drawing his pistol when Kurt stabbed him to death with a large metal file used for removing burrs from artillery rounds. Other workers kept up with their work on the noisy shop floor.

Kurt and I hid the body in a storage area outside where shavings were kept and every month or so sent to a smelter for meltdown.

———⌒———

A few weeks later two officers from camp administration assembled us on the shopfloor. I instantly knew why. I also knew what methods would be used.

One of the officers referred to the missing guard and stated he had no doubt that there were men in the room who knew what had befallen him. He tried to win our cooperation by saying he knew the guard to have been injudicious and sometimes cruel. His demeanor changed suddenly and he stated that if he did not have information on the matter at once, he would have no choice but kill every one of us.

Kurt whispered to me that he knew it would be a matter of time and that he knew what had to be done. He was resigned. I'd seen the look before. He handed me an envelope and asked that I get it to her. I promised I would, though of course we both knew that was unlikely. He thanked me then walked toward the SS officers.

In strong voice he admitted to killing the guard and hiding the body in a location he'd show them right away. The officers were proud that their methods had worked so well and so quickly.

As they escorted Kurt toward the storage area, a civilian technical consultant, Otto, spoke up. He insisted that Kurt was a productive worker but one who had become somewhat unbalanced in recent weeks. Otto took on a sympathetic look and said that the poor man had confessed to countless crimes. Otto had listened to him, feigned belief, then sent him back to work with a caution.

When Kurt insisted he could show them the body in the scrap shed, Otto laughed and said he went there every other day and there was no body there. "Poor fellow," Otto said sympathetically, "he means well but he's a little off balance. An excellent worker, though!"

Otto took them to the shed and showed them there was no body there and no evidence of a crime at the plant. The officers were baffled and went back to the administration building.

Otto later told Kurt and me that he didn't like cruel guards in his plant. Yes, discipline was important, but cruelty was beyond what was called for. It interfered with production schedules for which he had to answer with higher-ups.

I handed the letter back to Kurt.

My health continued to deteriorate. Fever, coughing. There was blood in my hand after an especially fierce coughing bout. The doctor told me there was nothing to be done but to keep my spirits up. He had to see a man that had been released from medical experiments. He's been subjected to rapid pressurization then depressurization and was now in bad shape.

"Brain damage, it would appear. He'll be assigned to pick up the dead for a few weeks. After that, who knows. The allies will be here soon. Keep your spirits up."

I lay back and went to sleep.

ANOTHER ESCAPE

T HE NEXT DAY I WAS able to eat breakfast. I rebounded somewhat, and I'm not sure why. That evening I sat with Dr Yanek and Leon. The doctor was frail and hopeless.

"I used to be a respectable doctor. Yes, I remember those days but I don't think I'll see them again."

Leon and I began to encourage him. He raised his hand to halt us.

"Your youth is what has brought you back, Herman. I am going to be fifty – tomorrow, I believe, or maybe the next day, or maybe yesterday. I can't sleep very well and when it comes, nightmares haunt me and bring me back to this. It's embedded in my soul. Even if I get out, which I doubt, I'll never be able to forget. We are all damaged goods."

Leon asked him to think of his family.

"Yes, I used to have a wife and a son. He was one year younger than you. They were sick when we arrived at Dachau and sent immediately to the unfit group. I am not sure that survival would be a good thing for me anymore."

I searched for words of hope but found none. Had I found them I couldn't have spoken them convincingly. Yanek had given his consent to begin the downward spiral.

Two days later, I believe in early December 1944, there was a selection. Typically selections were done quickly but this one was more thorough. We were divided into three groups. One group would stay in Dachau, another would be sent to another camp where workers were needed, the third group comprised the weak.

We waited our turns, naked, in the cold. Yanek and I looked at each other every few minutes as the line proceeded. He reached the stand and was told to cough, raise his arms, and bend down. A doctor placed a stethoscope to his chest, then sent him over to stand with the group to be sent to another camp for work.

I was next. I did the motions well and breathed in and out with the stethoscope to my chest. The doctor asked me to breathe in and out again.

"You've been sick, haven't you?"

"No, not at all. I've performed my work well."

He was unconvinced, he was uninterested. He motioned for me to go to the weak group.

"But I feel fit. I can do good work." I protested as spiritedly as I could and moved my arms about to demonstrate my health.

"Go!" He pointed once more to the walking dead.

I'd been sentenced to death. I trudged slowly to the group and looked around me. They were sick, extremely weak, and barely able to form rows. As much as I'd resigned myself to death someday, facing it that day was another thing. I reflected on my months of blank existence and realized that part of me still wanted to live. Memories of boyhood and play came to mind and they seemed to tell me I should have many years ahead of me. I wanted a way out.

Yanek attracted my attention not far from me, in the group designated for another labor camp. A quizzical look communicated that he didn't think I should be in the death group. I replied with a look of my own bewilderment.

Yanek shuffled nearer to my group and I inched toward his.

"Herman, switch places with me."

Initially puzzled, I soon comprehended, and shook my head.

"Take my place here, Herman. I'll take yours. I'm done here, remember?"

I shook my head again, though I must say parts of me insisted that I was younger than Yanek and in at least somewhat better health. A matter of poor judgment by an overworked doctor was all that kept me from his group, and he from mine.

"Switch places with me, Herman. It's what I want."

My look of sadness must have also conveyed acceptance and appreciation. I hope so. We waited a few moments until the guards looked toward the selection desks then in the blink of an eye, I was destined for another camp, he for death. We looked at each other and reached a silent understanding that I would make every effort to live through this. Yanek smiled.

"Move it!"

The kapos barked angrily and my group headed for the train tracks. Shortly later I heard the shriek of a whistle and in the distance, coming out of the morning fog, was a locomotive of the Death Express. I knew what it was pulling.

The train came to a halt and the cattle cars were opened. As we climbed in an SS guard mockingly said, "You're going to another place where work makes you free. This one is in Poland. *Auschwitz!*"

I almost laughed at the ghastly paradox of a return visit to Auschwitz. The presence of so many emaciated people held my dark humor in check. I wondered if the chances for this group were any brighter than those for the one Yanek was in now.

I thought of running, even though I knew I'd be shot down in an instant. Pushed on by the crowd, I climbed inside. We were packed in tighter than in my previous experiences on Eichmann's system. A few people died within hours.

I peeked through an opening and saw the German night, or was it a Polish night then? What became of Kurt and Leon? My mind vacillated between being grateful for life and returning to Auschwitz.

The slats were cracked and weakened, probably from previous travelers. One slat had been hastily nailed into position and with a little effort could be shoved away. I saw forests along the sides of the tracks and a familiar hope came to me. I showed the opening to the men around me but either through resignation or hope of better treatment ahead, they showed no interest in making for it. One shook his head and said he didn't want to die in a cold forest.

Though not in the best of health, I determined to make a try for it and waited for the train to slow for a curve. I made a final look for companions but saw continued disinterest. I squeezed through the slats and fell headlong onto the stony surface along the tracks, and rolled until I came to a graceless stop. Getting up on all fours, I felt around for broken bones and serious cuts. Happily, I found only scratches and sore areas that I knew would become large bruises.

I was free, but I was alone and had no idea where I was. I walked into the forest, covered myself with leaves and branches, and slept as well as anyone could.

The following morning I walked deeper into the forest. Which way should I go? Was there a friendly country nearby? Switzerland perhaps? Were there partisans in this forest?

I drank from a small stream and decided to follow its banks. Villages are on the banks of streams. So are borders. But so are government outposts for that matter.

I came across an old couple in a cabin atop a hill not far from the stream. They were milking goats and saw me before I saw them. They weren't alarmed so they did not recognize the significance of my pajamas, though they surely saw I wasn't in traditional peasant garb. Old and isolated from the cities, especially Berlin, they had no idea who or what I was. They gave me bread and told me which direction Switzerland was. "Toward the mountains," the old man said. They had no clothes to offer.

On I walked until I again covered myself with leaves and fell asleep. I was awakened by voices then a kick to my side. Men in uniforms, but not SS. In retrospect, they might have been border guards.

I was beaten, interrogated, then packed onto a train, judging by the sun, I was heading east, toward Poland. I was going back to Auschwitz after all.

THE ANGEL OF DEATH

B EATEN AND DAZED AND WORN down, I arrived late at night and was assigned to a temporary barracks. It had been a month and half or so since I escaped from the north end of Auschwitz-Birkenau, and now I was back. I saw the orderly lines of buildings, the tall fences with electrodes protruding from the posts, and the chimneys of the kremas.

Morning brought a selection and I had little doubt how I would fare. I was ready for it as I stood in line and listened to classical music through the public address system.

"Move along! Move along!"

I walked as best I could and stood in front of the medic. He was young and bored. I wondered if he thought his work contributed to the Reich. He took one look and motioned me over to the death group. No motions, no cough, no stethoscope.

There were over two hundred of us in an hour and we stood waiting, probably as one of the gas chambers was cleared. By the afternoon we began the march. Some cried, some prayed, most were silent. I didn't look at any faces. Guards and dogs surrounded us and we were herded toward one of the gas chambers at the north end.

My mind was blank. No weeping, no praying. I walked on with others. I didn't know any of them but in a few minutes I would share a horrible experience with them. The chamber was a hundred meters ahead. Some men were entering the anteroom.

Dark humor seized me. I will add that it buoyed me. It was an assertion of who I was in a dismal procedure that was going to kill me.

There's no place like home ... All roads lead to Auschwitz.
There's no place like home ... All roads lead to Auschwitz.
There's no place like home ... All roads lead to Auschwitz.

On I walked.

"Halt!"

The voice came from some distance. It wasn't one of the guards or kapos, but they stopped and of course so did we. An SS officer in a crisp immaculate uniform walked toward us, three SS guards around him brandishing machine pistols. The officer had dark hair and a confident demeanor. In another place, you might think him a good man. Here, he was another smiling Nazi.

"It is a day of good fortune for some of you!" He spoke calmly and almost gently. "I have openings in my section and some of you will come with me and serve in it."

He walked into the group and began inspecting us, starting with a boy nearby.

"Ach ... unfortunately you will not be one of them." He looked at another young man. "You I'm afraid are already gone."

He continued down the line then stopped at me.

"Stand straight."

I did.

"How old you?"

"Fourteen."

He nudged my arm with a baton to get me to raise it, then tapped my shoulder with it. "Turn around." He turned to his SS attendants and said, "He's surprisingly fit. Take him." He continued his inspection.

One of his guard's shoved me out of the death group. "You are the first one. He saved you! Come with me." He laughed at a joke I wasn't in on.

The officer selected a dozen of us, all boys and young men, and his guards marched us away toward nearby brick buildings. There was something puzzling about that SS officer. As we neared the building I asked the guard who the officer was. He smirked in a vulgar manner then jabbed me with the muzzle of his machine pistol, not nearly as hard as I'd expected. That too was puzzling.

"That was Dr Mengele. He is your savior this day."

The name meant nothing to me.

The guard looked at me as though enjoying a secret, and whispered. "Dr Mengele saved you but I have a feeling you'll regret he ever laid eyes on you." He laughed as he relished his joke all the more.

So, this Mengele fellow saved my life today.

We were taken inside one of the brick buildings. It was unexpectedly warm inside. A nurse led us to a dining hall which was smaller and neater than anything I'd seen since schooldays in Oradea. We were given plates with generous portions of bread and potatoes, and a cup of milk as well. It was bewildering, it was suspicious. I wondered if the Red Cross was coming again.

"Eat! You need to be strong." The nurse said.

She was young and pretty with delicate features, unlike the rather homely *Aufseherinnen* I'd catch glimpses of in the women's camps and elsewhere.

She pointed to the plate again. "Eat! You are severely malnourished. If you don't eat, you'll die."

I sent a weakened hand to the fork and began to eat.

Four of us were billeted in a small room with real beds, not the bunks we were packed into in the blocks. There was something strange. Yes, it was the presence of a powerful antiseptic smell which while not pleasant, was preferable to the stench of the blocks and covered up the lingering odor on us. The blanket was thin but softer to the touch than regular camp issue.

I lay down and looked up. No thick rafters, a plaster ceiling. I thought I was dreaming. In a moment I was sound asleep in a warm bed.

The same nurse woke us up in the morning.

"Get up! You need to eat breakfast. You'll also be treated for parasites. You'll feel better."

I didn't understand what she meant but her voice was so pleasant. She told us to follow her, and that we did.

"My name is Herman. May I ask yours?"

I just blurted it out. I have no idea how I summoned the courage or impertinence.

"My name is Anna. So strange . . . no one has ever asked me that."

She was as perplexed as I, but at least she wasn't angry. In fact she giggled.

"Why are you laughing?" I asked.

She didn't answer. Another inside joke, perhaps.

We were given a plate with eggs, sausage, and bread and butter. She instructed us to eat and without hesitation, we did.

"Small bites, young men. Small bites only."

I concluded my repast with a glass of milk. My courage or impertinence arose once more.

"How long have you worked here?"

"Oh . . . too long, I should think." Her face sank.

I was intrigued by, and welcomed, the thought of someone on the staff of Auschwitz troubled by the work. More than welcoming the idea, I marveled at it. She didn't fit here, and that was good.

"What is going to happen to me here?"

Anna looked at me even more sadly, then reverted to the role she was tasked to perform day after day at this theater. "You'll help us with medical experiments. It is for the greater good of the world. You'll help us make tremendous scientific advances."

It sounded so high-minded, it sounded so ominous.

I was taken to a room with medical equipment, including a rather large syringe which I judged, correctly as it turned out, was for me.

"Is this going to hurt?" I asked warily.

"Oh, Herman. . . ."

It did.

"Come, you'll need to take a shower and get hospital uniforms."

I took a shower with real soap and reasonably warm water. I was weighed. Thirty-five kilograms.

"You are very much underweight. But then, oh, so are all of you. So are all of you."

I was issued fresh clothing. It felt good to be clean again.

After a few hours of tests and paperwork. It was time for lunch. Chicken soup, with ample morsels of chicken. Bread and jelly. Two decent meals within a few hours.

"Today you'll meet our chief doctor. He'll talk with you personally and examine you. He's an expert in his field and we are fortunate to have him here."

The thought of a doctor was appealing. I remembered the doctors in Oradea and even in the camps. They were good souls, well trained and eager to help.

When I asked his name, Anna paused, "Dr Josef Mengele."

That name again. The man who took me from the line headed for the gas chamber. She retreated into detached officialdom. I was another patient once more. One of many who came and went.

Before my appointment, I was able to walk around a section of the building. I met a couple, husband and wife, a rarity in the camps as most were immediately separated on the platform. Hanna and Mendel were in their late twenties and cheerful, though they looked sickly, even stricken. They held hands and said it was a blessing that they were able to be together in the medical experiments. When Mendel said those words I felt he'd gone mad under the strain of the camp or from something he'd gone through in the building. Hanna looked much weaker than her husband.

When Anna returned, I asked her about them and instantly got a look of distance and regret.

"Hanna is sick and Mendel will be sick soon." She paused and seemed embarrassed. "But you know, Herman, this is for the greater good. It truly is. We will *all* benefit from this one day."

She saw my continued puzzlement and might have sensed my disappointment in her less than forthright response.

"Hanna has *cancer* and Mendel will have cancer soon."

I'd heard of cancer back in Oradea. The word had a dark aura around it in those days. A friend of Uncle Joseph had died of it. People didn't like to say the word and when they did, it was in whispers.

"How do you know that Mendel will soon have cancer?"

She was taken aback that a young boy would recognize the implication of her words.

"Because, Herman, we *gave* him cancer. They are part of a cancer experiment. Now we are testing a promising medicine on her. Soon, Mendel will also be quite ill."

"Has this medicine cured anyone?"

"No . . . no, I'm afraid not. Not yet. But we learn more everyday."

"So what's going to happen to her?"

"Her cancer has spread throughout her body. Nothing is likely to stop it at this point. Nothing. The same for Mendel, in all likelihood. But Dr Mengele is learning all the same, as is German science. And that is our purpose here."

She believed this. She believed in the building, in the institution, in the entire place. They did things for the good of mankind. All part of Hitler's plan.

"She is going to die, isn't she?"

"Yes, I'm afraid she is. But I am happy that the two are together. This is the end of their lives and although they didn't know that from the start, they know it now."

"So her husband is not far behind her with his disease, and he'll die also."

"I think so. Almost certainly."

She took pride in her professional assessment.

"Are they in pain?"

"Yes, but I must say they are the bravest patients I ever saw. They hardly complain and don't even ask for pain medication. Dr Mengele doesn't usually prescribe such things anyway. Mendel and Hanna just go on bravely. Being together gives them more time, and it gives us more time to learn from them."

I understood their expressions now. They knew they were gravely ill, and they were in pain, but at least they were together instead of being separated by a fence, worked hard, then murdered without the other's even knowing it. And their love for each other gave the Reich more information, useless though it likely was.

Years later, when I read Dante's *Inferno*, I imagined Auschwitz and Birkenau and Dachau as something like the rings of hell, each with parts more horrible than others, each reserved for special evildoers. Here, there were worksites of varying conditions and guards of varying cruelty. The worst ring was just north of the medical experiments building, and was complete with fires and chimneys. But unlike the condemned of Dante's vision, we'd done nothing to deserve our fates.

"What are you going to do to me?"

She shook her head. "I don't know yet. But I do know that Dr Mengele will see you this afternoon."

Anna brought me to an examination room and gave me a gown to put on. Minutes later Mengele entered with confident strides. He sat in front of me and looked into my eyes in a cheerful manner. No words, though he seemed eager to tell me something.

When he smiled I saw a gap between his front teeth. He exuded pride and energy. His brown eyes, however, had none of those things. I was struck by them. They were emotionless, detached from any human quality or emotion. They reminded me of the eyes of a dead fish staring blankly in a store window as it rotted. If eyes are the window to the soul, I was looking into the soul of death. I saw what lay behind every cattle car, block, kapo, guard, gas chamber, and crematory. If I'd encountered those eyes again decades later, in Europe or South America, I'd have recognized them.

"I am Dr Mengele. I understand that your name is Herman."

I nodded. Again that smile and those eyes.

"I also understand that you are from Oradea. That's what you told Anna."

"Yes."

"I'm sure it's lovely. Do you know what our mission is here, Herman?" he asked as he looked over his notes and jotted something down.

"Medical things?"

He again looked at me.

"Well, yes. Medical *research*, actually. We are conducting important research on many diseases. We are developing cures for them. They will help our Reich and the entire world. Do you like this idea?"

"Yes."

"Good, Herman, very good."

He made more notes.

"As you know, with every important endeavor, there is a reward. But then, there is also a price." He again looked into my eyes, about to gauge my response. "You and other people here will help us make important discoveries. That is the reward. The price . . . the price is *you*, Herman. Do you understand what I'm saying?"

I shook my head slowly. I thought of Hanna and Mendel.

"You will understand in time, Herman."

Then he asked me questions about my family, my medical history as well as that of my family, my education, and even if I ever had a girlfriend. He offered me a glass of water then gave me a brief physical. He seemed satisfied with what he saw.

"Well, Herman, you are in good shape. Frail and underweight, but this is the case in our camps." He almost looked embarrassed for a moment. "Are you going to help us here, Herman? Are you willing to cooperate with us?"

I nodded and wondered if he thought I had an alternative, besides the obvious, unattractive one.

"Excellent! Do you have any questions for me, Herman?"

I began to shake my head, but then I found myself saying I did have a question. He was surprised. It had probably never happened before. He sat back and waited intently for my question.

"The couple I met in the other room . . . Hanna and Mendel. They are sick with something that they got here. Do you make people sick here?"

How I came to ask that I don't know. Lingering exhaustion and unbridled curiosity? He was taken aback but quickly recovered.

"Remember that everything has a price, Herman. Yes, we have to give you and others diseases here. This is the only way we can experiment with new drugs and methods to find a cure. Do you understand now, Herman?"

"Yes . . . yes, but these people are going to die."

"Well, that's the price I referred to, and we must be willing to pay it."

The smile, the eyes. He wrote down a few more notes and strode out of the room.

Afterwards, I asked Anna what I would be put through. She avoided a meaningful answer.

Two or three days passed by uneventfully. It had been a week since Mengele took me out of the line of the dead, but I'd had no experiments done on me. I was being plied with food to restore my health. After that, there would be the price.

One night, just after dinner, Anna sat with me and watched me eat. She wasn't as engaging as usual. When I slowed my consumption, she urged me to finish my meal. She was biding her time, waiting for the proper moment.

"Tomorrow you'll start."

Her eyes were sorrowful. I might have reminded her of a younger brother.

"You've been chosen for a special experiment, one I've personally helped plan for you."

She saw anxiety pulse through me as I realized my vacation was coming to a close.

"Don't be alarmed, Herman. You'll not be injected with bacteria or the like. You will not be burned or immersed in frigid water.

You'll be testing the effect of closed-in places on people. That's your contribution to our work here."

"So, we start tomorrow then. I'm sure I'll be fine."

Anna nodded.

Over the following weeks, parts of my body – a hand, arm, or leg – were enclosed inside boxes for several days. After that, the containers became larger until I was completely enclosed in a metal case – a small coffin, one might say. I was unable to move much at all and there was no food or water for days. My only contact with the world was a tiny aperture above my face which enabled me to breathe and see light.

This was repeated several times. I became anxious, even terrified, and passed out after a day or two in my above-ground coffin. When at length I was let out, Anna was there with food and water. After a few days of recovery, another session began.

As strange as it may sound, I became accustomed to the procedures. I knew when they'd begin and in general terms at least, how along they'd last. I did not experience severe pain, only great anxiety. There was no vicious kapo or sadistic guard, there was Anna.

Naturally, a reluctance to place myself in a confined area has stayed with me. To this day, stairways are much preferred to elevators. Not as fearsome a price as I expected, nor nearly as fearsome as many paid in Mengele's medical buildings. I have no idea what purpose the box experiments served.[6]

Sometime during that period, I turned fifteen.

I usually ate by myself during my time in the medical buildings. Other people were nearby, of course, but I liked having my meals on my

---

[6] An inquiry to Yad Vashem was unable to figure out any purpose, either.

own. Sometimes Anna was nearby. I think she wanted to chat with me at times but had to maintain official distance.

One evening I heard Anna's footfalls followed closely by those of someone else's. She entered the mess hall with a boy about my age. Looking at his emaciated frame, I could see that he was no newcomer to Auschwitz. She led him over to where I sat.

"Herman, this is Yitzhak."

He and I looked at each other but did not speak.

"Yitzhak will be in your section for a while. Like you, he has to gain some strength before he'll be able to help us."

We shook hands briefly and smiled even more briefly. Anna was moved, though in a sad way. I had some idea of what went on here, but I sensed he knew nothing. Anna had a meal placed before Yitzhak and urged him to eat. Uncomfortable, she left.

Yitzhak looked in amazement at the sizable portions before him and the clean well-lit hall we were in. I had the same reaction when I arrived.

"Go on, eat, Yitzhak. It's all for you. But eat slowly, otherwise you'll get stomach aches. I should know. I ate fast at first and had trouble for several days."

Even as I was speaking those words I knew he wouldn't heed them. Inmates were simply too hungry and once we took a bite, an urge to devour all before us set in. And that's what happened right before me. Yitzhak took a bite of bread, then another. Then it was on to the wurst and whatever else was on the plate. He was working on the crumbs and morsels in less than five minutes. As a finishing touch, he licked the plate, as a child might be urged to do by parents.

When he looked at me almost apologetically, I repeated that I'd done the same thing.

He was from Oradea and naturally we spoke of schools and friends, though we determined that we had none in common. My estimation of him increased when he said he loved soccer. Thirteen, an only child, he and his parents had been in the Oradea Mare ghetto and were separated on arrival at Auschwitz. By then, he knew what that meant. I don't think he clung to any hope.

After a few minutes of silence, Yitzhak asked what I knew he would ask the moment Anna left.

"What will they do to me here?"

I wasn't going to mislead him. That would put me on the other side. I told him that it was medical research – very dangerous medical research. Some lived, some didn't. No, most didn't.

He nodded. That's all. He knew enough about the camp to know there was no good place in it, only less terrible ones. Anna returned and took him to his room.

———

After a week of rest and decent meals, Yitzhak's part in Mengele's research began, and I didn't see him. I learned he was undergoing the same confinements that I was.

Shortly thereafter, Anna led him into the mess hall. He was trembling badly. His eyes were red and swollen from terror. His procedures might not have begun as benignly as mine had. I patted his hand to calm him and urged him to eat.

"It was bad, Herman."

That was all Yitzhak could say. He didn't have to say anything. His anguish and terror were clear.

I told him it would get easier then changed the subject to places in Oradea.

———

His second session went better, his third better still. We ate meals together when we could. He talked of a girl named Sara he was especially fond of. It was good for both of us. Try as I did to avoid emotional ties, Yitzhak was becoming my friend.

"Do you think we'll live through this?" he asked one night after dinner.

"I don't really know. I suppose it's possible."

"I want to leave this place someday. I want to see Sara again. She's a year older than I am but that's no obstacle. She's so lovely and life is beautiful with her. I hope to marry her one day."

It was sweet, it buoyed him. He never mentioned where she was then and I didn't ask. I mentioned hope of playing soccer again on green fields far away. I talked about Focsani and hoped that things were better for my parents and siblings there.

My companion had no family left.

Yitzhak and I went on different schedules, and we ate at different times. Anna came in.

"Herman, I want to tell you something. Dr Mengele has selected Yitzhak for other experiments."

"What type of experiments?"

"We'll know more soon. You might see a change in his behavior and I wanted you to know that."

Anna saw my concern and for a moment I saw hers. But she wanted no more questions and retreated into officialdom.

"Finish your meal and go to your quarters – and please tell your friend of the change in routine."

Ah, so that's what this was about.

Yitzhak and I ate together soon thereafter. We chatted as I bided my time. He provided the opportunity by asking why I was so pensive.

"There's been a change. You're going to be part of new experiments."

He was instantly dismayed.

"What kind?"

"I don't know, Yitzhak. I only know they will be different. Maybe they'll be easier."

"Maybe. . . ."

I told him that he'd already been through a lot and he would have to continue being strong. He smiled bravely and told me he would.

I hadn't seen Yitzhak for a week until an evening Anna led him into the mess hall. He walked slowly and unsteadily. She helped him sit near me then left. His eyes were vacant. I started to greet him but saw he was still elsewhere. He stared ahead blankly. I thought he was replaying in his mind what had happened to him during the last few days. Over and over.

"Yitzhak . . . Yitzhak. . . ."

He remained in the past. He took no food.

I looked to Anna for explanation.

"He's been like this for a few days. Dr Mengele thought you could bring him out of it."

I had no interest in helping Mengele, of course, but I wanted to help Yitzhak. I spoke his name several times, sometimes insistently, other times pleadingly. He remained unresponsive.

Disappointed, and I believe saddened, Anna looked on from another table.

I renewed my efforts to reach Yitzhak. I asked him questions about Oradea and specific places in the city. I asked about Sara, but there was still no connection. After quite some time, I simply asked,

"What did they do to you? What did they do to you, Yitzhak?"

His eyes were still vacant but they blinked, as though trying to come back or at least to send a message that part of him was still here. I placed a spoonful of soup to him and he took it in, sipping slowly and swallowing. I continued this, all the while talking to him, until he'd ingested most of the meal.

Anna, for one reason or another, was pleased. She patted me on the back.

"He eats, but he's not here with us, Anna."

"He's in there somewhere. I hope he feels safe there."

———

Not long thereafter, she again brought Yitzhak to the mess hall. I tried anew to reach him but was unable to repeat even my meager results from the last time. Oradea . . . Sara. . . . Nothing could get him back. I did manage to get a few spoonfuls of nourishment into his system.

There was no sign of beatings or any other physical injury. His remoteness was quite different from the resignation I'd seen on those who'd given up. They trudged along and occasionally spoke. Poor Yitzhak was further away. I thought Mengele's experiments were damaging his brain.

A few days after that, Anna brought him to me once more. No response. I couldn't manage to get him to ingest a single bite, only a small amount of water. Anna said the Mengele had been injecting him with an experimental medicine. I'm not sure even she knew just what it was or what it was supposed to do.

The next evening Mengele observed us in the mess hall. I was unable to elicit any response. Mengele said to Anna in a matter-of-fact way, "He's of no further use."

I came to see Anna in much less human terms than I once did. She was part of this. She worked for Mengele. I avoided looking at her.

One evening she came in alone.

"Herman? Herman?"

There was a quaver in her voice.

"Herman, in a few days Dr Mengele will send Yitzhak away from here. He's done here."

For some days I'd known he was doomed, but hearing the hour was close sickened me.

"Herman," her voice became official. "Listen to me. It's not in my power to change anything. I'm not the decision maker. I'm a nurse. Yitzhak is leaving here. Listen Herman, I want to suggest something."

I wondered what she wanted from me now.

"Yitzhak will have one more meal here this evening. He will be sent away in the morning. You can help him. I'll give you a cup of juice and I want you to help him drink it."

My look of incomprehension must have been obvious.

"This will be a special drink. One with *medicine*. It's the best thing. Do you understand? He'll simply fall asleep."

I understood. I understood that Yitzhak's dreams of soccer and Oradea and Sara would end as he fell asleep. And he would leave Auschwitz.

"It's the best thing, Herman. I'll get him now."

Anna brought Yitzhak into the now empty mess hall. I tried to reach him, though I knew it was pointless. Efforts to get him to eat were no more successful. I looked into Yitzhak's eyes, though his gaze went straight through me.

"Yitzhak my friend, tomorrow morning you will be sent to the gas chamber. I wish I had better news, but there isn't any here tonight. I have juice that will put you to sleep, forever. It's better this way, Yitzhak. You have to help me. You have to drink it."

His eyes blinked several times.

It was a sign. Yitzhak was giving his consent.

I lifted the cup to his mouth and he took a few cautious sips. I raised the cup higher until its contents were gone.

Amazing. Sickening.

Anna thanked me and started to take Yitzhak away.

"Can he stay here with me a while?"

"Yes, but not long. It's better that he be in his bed."

I sat there with him for some time, my hand resting on his. I said farewell to Yitzhak and watched him walk away unsteadily with Anna's help.[7]

Hanna and Mendel's health and spirits fluctuated. They told me of their love for music, especially the violin and piano. They were given instruments to play for the entertainment of the medical staff. One night I was in attendance. So was Mengele. I sat far away.

---

[7] In retrospect, I'm uncertain what it was that Mengele had been injecting into Yitzhak that put him into that state. It's possible that there was some research involved. But so much of what went on there had no relationship to medicine. Mengele simply enjoyed inflicting pain and illness on people, until they were of no further use.

Hanna played the violin, Mendel the guitar. It was lovely. It was also a jarring paradox. There in the room were men and women who conducted procedures that inflicted terrible pain and death, but who were now enjoying a delicate piece of classical music, as though in a fashionable drawing room in Berlin or Vienna. Those men and women were having a social hour, as would employees of a government bureau or a manufacturing concern. Laughter and gayety, conversation and flirtation.

A violin tucked beneath her chin, Hanna's face conveyed passion and occasional discomfort. She lost her timing and began to play ahead of her husband. She was immersed in the music. Mendel tried to catch up but never found the right place. She'd conclude one piece and the instant a patter of applause began, she'd start another.

Timing gone, her performance became frenzied. Mendel stopped completely – I think out of concern. Then she called out his name, dropped the violin to the floor, and slumped over into his arms.

"Mendel, hold me! Please hold me!"

"I'm here with you."

"I'm going away, Mendel. Please kiss me."

Hanna was succumbing to the experiments that people in that room had forced on her. It was clear to all. The doctors did not rush to her side. They watched as though it was part of a research lecture or a scene from a familiar play. Perhaps they planned an autopsy in the morning.

I was moved by the scene. I thought her better off.

One doctor said, "Such a shame. The concert was going so well."

And with that, the staff filed out of the room, probably disappointed that the show was over. Mengele remained. He approached Mendel as he continued to hold his wife.

"She was a fine musician."

Mengele spoke without a trace of sympathy or any other human emotion.

"I can't live without her," Mendel whimpered.

"Ah, but you won't have to."

There was neither spite nor intended cruelty. It was simply how Mengele related to us. He could be engaging and even affable, but our deaths were of no more significance than that of a small insect.

Mendel was incredulous at the heartlessness. He glared at Mengele, conveying his contempt and hatred more than any words could. Mengele didn't care about meaningless issue from the nerve tissue of a small insect. He turned and left the room. That was the last time I saw him.

A few of us, including Anna, helped carry Hanna's body to the couple's room, and gently place her on the bed. Mendel folded her hands across her front. I stood silently for a moment. Anna offered Mendel a medicine cup. He looked at it briefly, then thanked her.

I said how sorry I was. Another death in one of the dark blocks or a worksite or a shower room would not have affected me. Not much anyway. But here in the surreal medical experiments building, Hanna's death hurt me.

He drank the medicine then shook my hand. "Take care, Herman my friend. Take care." Mendel then lay down next to Hanna.

I sat in my quarters, bewildered by the events of the last hour. Anna came to apprise me of the following day's schedule.

"We'll never see them again, will we."

"Go to sleep, Herman. New things are coming tomorrow. I do not know if they are good or bad, but I hope they are good for you. I simply don't know anymore. Sometimes I think that anywhere is better than here, but only time will tell."

Anna stopped as she reached the doorway. Without facing me she said, "No, Herman, we'll never see them again."

I couldn't sleep. I kept thinking of Hanna and Mendel playing music together. I fell asleep only very late.

Anna woke me up, obviously worried.

"You are all being taken away. I don't know where to."

I had an immediate guess.

"All the staff here is packing up and going to another camp. I must pack as well, so I cannot stay long. Put this bread in your pocket. And you must change back into the striped uniform."

She was near tears.

"Herman, I don't know how to say this. . . ." Her voice quavered and tears fell. "I'm very sorry for what's happened to you and others here. I wish I could stop it." She looked around the room as though a way might come to her.

"I know, Anna."

Strangely, I think she cared about me, as if I reminded her of a younger brother – or of a boy my age who'd come to the building, stayed a while, then paid the price. Was it by chance that I was spared from lethal experiments? Yes, someone on Joseph Mengele's staff had grown fond of me, and I of her. So strange what life shows us.

"Oh, Herman. Seeing Hanna and Mendel over the last few weeks saddened me so. Many times I offered them something to end their pain, and many times they refused. He said once that it was against his religion to commit suicide. Last night I told him it was medicine."

It sank in and fit with my suspicions. A moment of decency intermingled with death.

"But he knew."

She hugged me, as though I was her only source of light left.

"I have to take you and the others out to the yard now."

"Am I. . . ?"

"No. You're going to another camp. You take care of yourself, Herman. It won't be long now."

I left the paradoxical safety of Mengele's building and stood in the January cold. Back again in prison issue, I took my place in the long, silent rows and columns with hundreds of others and listened to classical music from the speakers, as I had so many times before.

That morning, there might have been many thousands of us. I looked for familiar faces, especially Yanosh's, but without success. I thought how twisted this world is, and wondered what lay ahead.

DEATH MARCH

MENGELE'S BUILDINGS WERE WARM. I must say that. Out in the field, the bitter cold ran through my uniform and pierced me as though a thousand razors. My teeth chattered noisily. We stood for hours, far more than I'd ever experienced.

Roll calls were usually organized events. There was work to be done and German efficiency prevailed, even in southern Poland. There was less order that morning. A few men fell to the ground. I tore off pieces of bread from my pocket and surreptitiously chewed them. Fuel for my furnace.

Finally, an SS officer addressed us.

"We have received urgent orders to move to another camp – a work camp in the fatherland. There we shall continue to help in the war effort and ensure many more victories to come. We shall depart momentarily."

"Lying bastard! You are losing the war."

An odd, emaciated man in his thirties, eyes sunk into his skull like most of us, muttered not far from me. He saw my interest.

"Germany is losing, I tell you. The Russians are drawing closer and closer. They are well into Poland and will soon be in his precious *fatherland*. That is why we are being moved."

"How do you know?"

"I have ways of knowing."

He wasn't in a striped inmate uniform. For some reason he wore dark blue work clothing. The stubble of his beard seemed glued to his face. When he spoke it was clear he'd lost a few teeth over the years or months. It all contributed to a crazed look. I thought he had broken from reality altogether and had fled into an inner world of fantasy, like that affluent woman in the cattle car who laughed about going to Lublin.

"I am Benjamin. And you, young man?"

"Herman."

"Where were you working?"

"I was in the medical experiments building."

"Oh, dear God. . . ." He looked at my face and shoulders. "You seem well, though. Most don't come out."

"Yes, I was lucky." If I'd told him of my protective nurse, he'd have thought I was the crazed one.

"I heard about this. The Nazis are moving Jews to camps inside Germany because they are losing the war and need labor for a final defense. What great news!" I can't recall seeing more joy in an inmate. "We have to get through this journey into his fatherland. We must. I'll tell you two things. First, the journey won't be short, and second, they'll give us no food on it."

Long march, no food. I looked around and wondered how many of us would fall along the way, with an SS guard to finish the job from a shot or two. Then I thought they'd want to save every round for the Russians.

"How do they expect to get us into Germany?" I asked.

"That's exactly the point. They don't."

I began to think Benjamin was one of the inmates who prided himself on great knowledge – the inside dope, as they say – but who only had heard a rumor or two and elaborated upon them until they'd become veritable dogma.

"It's another one of their ways to kill more of us. Death by long marches – in the January cold. I worked with a man that was on one such march and had the good fortune to survive it. We will be on a *death* march, boy. We are about to walk a great distance in order to kill off the weak."

It made sense. Clearly, the camps were designed to kill us, either through labor, malnutrition, beatings, bullets, or gas. Someone in an office somewhere had plotted a new method. Men who killed small children with poison gas or by smashing their skulls would look upon a death march as one of their less brutal and less memorable endeavors. I felt how much bread I had in my pocket and wondered how far I had to go.

"Mark this day well, boy. This is the day that you started off on the death march. I don't know where we are going but we will make it. I intend to survive this damn war. I was an historian in Munich and I'll be an historian again when this is over. I'll be there to write about it. There's so much to document, so much. I'll remember it all."

I looked at him more and saw another scarecrow of a man whose face wrapped tightly around the bones of his head. How many had I seen fall down, or get sent into the line for the north end of Birkenau, or run out and grab the wire? But I started to see his look not as crazed, but as determined. It fascinated me and I decided that when the time came, I'd give him some of the food Anna gave me.

Prior to departure there was a quick selection. A few hundred were spared the travails of the road by being gassed to death. Shortly thereafter we marched out of Auschwitz-Birkenau.

It felt good to be out of there, despite my partner's foreshadowing. Instead of rows of bleak barracks and administrative buildings and vicious guards, I saw tree-lined lanes, rural villages, and simple farmers. It was almost pleasant, relatively speaking of course. Only at first, though.

The cold cut though us, so we bunched together to fend off the wind as best we could, and kept up a pace to circulate thin blood through weak bodies, though we had to slow considerably after a few hours. Many could not keep up or fell to the ground. SS soldiers, some in military vehicles, some on foot, finished them off. Loud reports could be heard every half hour or so.

Benjamin walked without any difficulty and again I wondered where his power came from. He marched along with a fierce look. "These bastards will not defeat me." I think he was writing lecture notes and chapter outlines in his mind. He looked to me and grinned. "You also have to hold on, boy. Hold on. Freedom is almost here." And so we walked on, ever to the west.

I handed him a chunk of bread. He was amazed.

"You must have a guardian angel above you, boy." He smiled and hurriedly crammed the bread into his mouth. I did not give account of my guardian angel-like benefactor.

The march went into the night, and all through it. In the morning gray, we entered a village. Road signs indicated we were still in Poland. A few people were up and out. They stopped and stared at us as though we were ghastly apparitions from the beyond. Indeed, that is how we must have looked – grimy wraiths in tattered clothing, trudging along country roads, escorted by pitiless guards who themselves must have resembled the worst criminals of Germany, Poland, and the Ukraine.

Some of the villagers looked upon us with sorrowful eyes and tried to hand us food and water. But the SS shouted at them to stop, saying we were Jews and deserved no favors.

One woman was splendidly dressed, as though on her way to a religious service or town social. She was stunned and made a point to look at individuals as they filed by. As we reached her, Benjamin smiled and bowed courteously. He even pretended to tip his hat, as though conveying his regards for the new day. She understood his dark humor and smiled wanly.

Another day of the death march was coming to a close. I was near collapse. SS guards came by intermittently and I continued to hear rifle shots. I'd lost feeling in my toes and most of my body. As night fell once more, we were unable to see more than a few feet ahead of us. We simply followed the fellow in front of us and put one foot out in front of the other.

I looked over to Benjamin and told him I couldn't go on anymore. I was done for.

"Yes you can, boy." His voice was more stern than encouraging. "You must. You must show them."

I pushed on. I couldn't see well anymore. It wasn't simply the night. My vision was failing. What little glimmers of moving objects I saw were badly blurred.

The temptation to fall and just lay on the ground was strong, though I knew my rest would have ended with a swift dispatch into nothingness. I pressed forward with my dwindling powers. I daydreamed of a soft, warm, white bed on which I'd sleep an entire weekend. So pleasant, so appealing – so distracting. I tripped and started to fall. A hand reached out from the dark and pulled me up. It was Benjamin, of course. He supported me for a few more moments until I was able to get back into my rhythm. I was too weak to thank him.

Amid my daze I wondered what force in the world gave him such strength. I was unable to think clearly, of course, but there was a vast reservoir of energy near me upon which I could draw as needed.

At length we arrived at the city of Wodzislaw, about fifty miles from Auschwitz. We were allowed to sit on the ground as the SS performed another quick selection. Those judged too weak were shot. The rest of us were packed into cattle cars and sent across the border into Germany. We soon came to a halt at a camp called Gross-Rosen.[8]

---

[8] On January 18th, 1945, tens of thousands of inmates began the Death March from Auschwitz and its many sub-camps to Gross-Rosen and other sites. About twenty-five percent perished along the way.

GROSS-ROSEN

W E ARRIVED LATE AT NIGHT and were immediately allocated into the main camp and several sub-camps. Surprisingly, we were given something to eat. It was only tasteless soup but it was warm and gave energy.

We were assigned to long blocks, all of a similar design as elsewhere. Inside were the familiar wooden bunks and straw mattresses. After the long march in the cold and the intermittent executions, the barracks were a welcome sight. The straw was quite dry and we were not as crammed in as at Auschwitz and Dachau. We later learned that these blocks were recent additions to the camp and that the other ones were as bad if not worse than the previous places the Reich had seen fit to place me.

The next morning we were assigned to work kommandos. The regimen at Gross-Rosen was very harsh. The extreme cold and twelve-hour workday made for extremely high mortality rates, especially after the long march. The hope that anyplace would be better than Auschwitz faded.

Benjamin and I were assigned to a granite quarry. I knocked away loose material from immense slabs. Benjamin split large stones and ground them into construction material. Very difficult work. Very dangerous too.

Every morning at breakfast, Benjamin was nonetheless optimistic. Liberation was at hand. He had no doubt.

"We are almost there. It is February and I hear the winds of freedom blowing more strongly everyday, from east and west."

Beneath his grimy beard I could see a confident smile. He never ceased to impress me.

"I'm an historian! I have to survive to tell of this. It's my duty. Just wait and see. I will write a thick book about everything my eyes have seen and everything my body and soul have endured. Ah, my book will be amazing!"

I was in awe of his perseverance and sense of mission. Yes, a man drove himself to survive in order to document this. He amazed me. He gave me strength.

The SS became more abusive. They beat us more and cut our rations. Deaths were increasingly common. We thought the increased brutality was the result of steady losses on the war fronts and imminent defeat. The rumors of the Red Army closing in were encouraging. The Russians took on heroic hues in our minds and at night I'd listen for rumblings from the east.

One of our tasks at the quarry was heaping granite into large metal bins that were then hoisted out of the excavation pit by an immense crane which creaked and groaned as it slowly lifted its cargo high into the air. The guards enjoyed ordering some of us to stand beneath the heavy bins as they went skyward. If the material dropped for one reason or another, those below would be crushed to death. And of course the rules of the game stipulated that anyone who raced away would be shot immediately.

One day, an obese and sickly guard ordered us to place a greater quantity of granite than usual into a bin. The more weight, the greater danger. He knew it, we knew it. A half dozen of us were ordered to stand beneath the bin as it began its ascent. The crane groaned and creaked far more loudly than before. We looked skyward as the machinery protested the greater burden.

Machinery and cable suddenly fell silent. The bin slowed to a halt above us, swaying back and forth menacingly. The engine above sputtered back to life then backfired loudly before quitting again. A moment later the bin began to come down in awkward lurches. A safety mechanism kicked in and slowed it, but the descent continued and indeed accelerated.

"Stay right where you are," the guard chortled amid coughing bouts, rifle at the ready.

As I stood there with tons of rock descending on me, and a guard eager to shoot me, well, I thought a fifteen-year-old boy would become another nameless corpse. I shouted out to no one in particular.

Two things took place within seconds. The guard's chortling turned into uncontrolled coughing. He grabbed his chest, and his face reddened and showed clear signs of distress then alarm. He was struggling for air. No one rushed to his aid, needless to say. We were still afraid to leave our position beneath the bin. Besides, our compassion for fellow humans wasn't limitless.

"I'm coming!" A voice called out from high above us. I looked up into the sunlight and saw a man racing to the crane. He grabbed a lever near the immense gears and pulled with all this might. More growling metal and squeaking cables, but the bin kept moving. The man then placed himself into the gear mechanism and let the cogs slowly pull him in, crushing him, but jamming the machinery, and bringing the bin to a halt.

With the guard clearly incapacitated, a few of us clambered up the walkway to the rim of the pit to see what could be done for the man. It was Benjamin and he was hideously mangled in the machinery. Blood was coming from his mouth as his lungs and stomach had been pierced by broken ribs. We tried to extricate him but could not.

I looked to him as though asking why.

"I don't know, Herman . . . I don't know."

Again I looked to him, and again he understood.

"I'll not write my history after all."

He looked down at his grotesquely disfigured body and wryly said, "My day has been ruined." He looked up at me and whispered, "Take care, my boy."

And with that, he was gone.

"Out of the way! Out of the way!"

SS guards were racing to the scene.

"What do we have here? What happened, boy?"

I gave a brief reply then he looked to Benjamin.

"Ah, I knew that Jew. He was a hard worker."

Benjamin had at least a little value to him.

"He died saving you scum? Not worth it, old fool, not worth it. All of you, back to work. We'll get the crane back in operation soon."

We left Benjamin's remains in the gears and returned to work. Later that day a team of engineers repaired the crane. The SS told me and another boy to toss Benjamin's body in the pile of dead not far from the pit. We'd put corpses there before; death was by our side as we worked. We laid him on the ground near a tree and arranged him to appear as though he was sleeping. It was an effort to give him final dignity.

I sank into depression, again. I performed my labor, ate with indifference, and spoke to others as little as possible. I'd loved Benjamin, and wanted no more of the sorrows that came with that emotion. I came to think that love had no reason to be in Nazi camps, and that it was only a pleasant illusion outside of them. I thought of Benjamin's reason for existence, of his request, and of my feeble, unspoken promise to remember.

Cold and alone in Gross-Rosen, shivering beneath a thin blanket, I thought back to my boyhood in Oradea, the ghetto, and the camps I'd been at over the last eight months. I'd never forget those events, though I wished I could. Yes, they should be written down somewhere, someday, someplace – someplace far from Germany and Poland. I thought it might serve as some sort of documentation and also as a warning. I was able to sleep.

It was March 1945 and everywhere there was talk that the Third Reich would soon fall. We were assembled in the main yard of Gross-Rosen where the commandant informed us of another move. Another death march. He noted that those unable to make the march would be shot, so we braced ourselves for the effort. I thought back to the march of just a few weeks earlier and put my mind in the routine of placing one foot in front of the other. A misstep and I might not be able to get back up.

We were issued a ration of bread and a substance resembling butter, then we marched out of Gross-Rosen. Our destination was unknown to us. As I thought, we marched west, away from the Russian army, deeper into Germany. I wondered how far away the Americans and British were.

The march lasted several days, longer than the one from Auschwitz to Wodzislaw in January. The elements, the hunger, and the exhaustion took a predictably heavy toll. SS guards herded us, others raced by in vehicles.

The roadsigns were in German now. Simple villagers came out to look at the march of the emaciated, the parade of cadavers. Again I saw sympathy on the faces of onlookers. So it wasn't Germans I should hate, only Nazis. I marched with that thought, step after step, mile after mile.

Finally, we came to another camp.

I was wrong a few months back as I walked to the gas chamber. All roads do not lead to Auschwitz. This road had led me to Dachau, again.

DACHAU, AGAIN

I T WAS BEWILDERING AND DISPIRITING to be back there. As we trudged through the gates I recognized buildings and yards and walls. Why was fate taking me back and forth between Auschwitz and Dachau? I was trapped on an immense broken record.

Why? I asked myself over and over. Hardly an original question in those days. No answer arrived.

My dark humor came to my aid. I thought to myself that the Third Reich should have the consideration to show me one of their many other camps. I laughed at this – not inside to myself, but aloud. Those near me looked over, then went back to the march into Dachau. I appeared to be another case of someone who'd endured too much and was now breaking down into private madness. I thought of Lublin.

It was quite the opposite. My dark humor, which has stayed with me to this day, and which I consider an integral part of me, kept me from falling to the ground in private madness, before being shot. I was mastering the situation by asserting Herman Rittman over it, by placing his stamp on it, then putting one foot out in front of the other. Dark humor makes you free.

As we were led to our new barracks I noticed a change. The SS guards and officers were not focused on intimidating us. The first hours at a camp usually saw shouting and beating and occasional summary murders. Nothing like that this day. We were placed into a block and left alone. No one inspected us, no one ordered us into the bunks.

I sat on a mildewy wooden shelf and listened to men talk about the new place and the odd laxity and the imminent end to the war. One spoke quietly and cynically.

"I stopped believing in this end of the war talk long ago. I've heard it for too long and nothing ever comes of it."

He was another living skeleton. Sunken eyes, grimy uniform. Probably mid-twenties. I likely looked like a somewhat younger version of himself.

"I'm Herman Rittman."

"Juda Shapher. How long were you in Gross-Rosen?"

"Not long. A few weeks. We were marched there from Auschwitz."

"Ah, and you survived it. Happy?"

I didn't understand the question. Happy? My puzzlement must have been clear.

"Were you happy you survived the march? Or would you prefer to have died somewhere along the way?"

"No, surviving was good fortune. A friend helped me persevere. He died in a quarry at Gross-Rosen. An amazing man . . . an historian. I'm fortunate to have come across him in any circumstances."

Juda was neither moved nor interested. I better understood his question. He was bitter and cynical.

"You know, based on what I see here now, I believe the war is truly nearing an end – a bad one for Germany and for these guards here."

Juda was interested only in my naivety.

"Oh, please explain to me how you arrived at your cheerful conclusion."

"I was here a few months ago and the place is very different. The guards were more energetic, enthusiastic, and how to say it. . . ."

"More murderous?" Juda completed.

"Yes, they did kill more of us back then. They were eager to do their killing because they had faith in the Reich and in victory. Now? They've lost hope. It's *they* who've lost hope. It's on their faces and in the way they no longer enforce rules like lights out. They just took us here and left us."

He waved his hand dismissively. "Ah, that's simply because we arrived at night. Tomorrow they'll butcher us as usual, and you'll feel at home again."

At least he had dark humor.

"Maybe, maybe not. New people have heard the news. They say the Russians are coming from the east, and the British and Americans are coming from the west. The Germans are losing. They're on the run."

"And the new people are correct."

A new voice, one of an older man. He came over to us.

"I am Moritz. Yes, the allies are closing in, but that's all the more reason to be alarmed."

My boyish face displayed no sign of comprehension.

"The Nazis are ordering these death marches from all their camps. They want to destroy evidence of what they've been doing over the years. Buildings can be blown up, bodies can be buried or burned. But us – we are living evidence, witnesses. We can put nooses around their necks."

"So they want us all dead."

"Exactly, young man. But their plan won't succeed. There are too many of us. Some of us will get though these last weeks and we will tell the story."

"I wouldn't count on it. They are very efficient at killing large numbers of people. They've mastered the process." It was Juda, of course.

"I'm only saying that we need to follow their orders and keep a low profile for the next few weeks, until we're liberated. It's April – spring time."

I nodded.

"You talk as though we cause trouble wherever we go! We obeyed – always. We kept low – always. And did it help? No! We were beaten and killed. I agree with what you say about killing all the witnesses, but they are too clever, too fiendish. They'll find a way to kill us just before their Reich comes crashing down. It's in their plan. It's in their Wagner. Mark my words. I'm going to sleep now. My plan, friends, is not to make a plan. I may only live until tomorrow morning."

With that, Juda was off.

Moritz and I watched him climb onto his wooden bunk.

"I've seen many like him. Go to sleep, Herman. We have a mission for the next few weeks – surviving the next few weeks!"

It was time for me to nod off. I reached for my blanket and remembered I hadn't been issued one.

The next morning we were assigned to work in an armaments factory. It was not the same one that I worked at on my first time at Dachau. This was a smaller plant that made machine-gun parts. The machinery was designed for very low tolerances so as to make the weapons more lethal. The plant wasn't operating at capacity. Far from it. Things were winding down.

I tried to learn information about Kurt, my fellow inmate who'd been with the White Rose, but was unable to find out anything.

There was only one civilian engineer and one SS guard, though at times even the guard was absent. We had time to talk about the end of the war and what might happen afterwards. However, we were mindful of the warnings that we could all be massacred. All we could do was stick to our routine.

One morning we were assembled in the yard, as usual. We stood there longer than usual, though. At least it was no longer winter.

"Something is wrong," Moritz whispered. "We should have been marched to work by now."

I felt uneasy too.

After a long period of nervous waiting we were ordered to form rows and columns. Fifty of us, flanked by guards, marched away from the assembly yard and then outside the fences of Dachau. Well behind us were a pair of guards towing a large weapon mounted on a chassis with two wheels. I'd never seen one before.[9] I looked for an opportunity to make a run for it but there were too many guards with machine pistols.

We marched to a small hill in a wooded area. Below I could see a swift-moving stream which might take me swiftly away from there, if I could reach it. We were ordered to march down the slope and line up along the bank. I looked over to Moritz and he seemed resigned. He whispered goodbye to me. I thought of all the people I'd known who'd been killed one way or another, and of Benjamin's desire to write his book.

The SS officer finished speaking with his sergeants and stood in a manner of a man about to read a verdict.

"Today, work will be here in the forest. You will cut down trees and bring firewood to the camp. Implements will arrive shortly. Anyone trying to escape will be shot."

Guards began to feed an ammunition belt into that monstrous gun and with a loud click, the first round was chambered. If any of us made a run for it, the shooting would start immediately, beginning with the escapees. Behind me a pastoral image of a Bavarian stream complete with ducks. Before me, an SS detail determined to eliminate witnesses. It was so warm and sunny.

Nazi propaganda about the Jews taking over Germany came to mind. I'd once asked my uncle why those lies were told and he replied that such things had always been part of history. Here I was in another chapter in that history and in the final act of a Nazi play.

Fifteen years of life and I hadn't had the opportunity to do much. I thought about all the things that I could have done – learning a skill related to cars, and of finding love and raising a family. Behind me, the ducks. Before me, the SS. I thought what a dreadful world I lived in.

---

[9] Many years later I determined the weapon might have been a Flugabwehrkanon 38 – a 20mm antiaircraft gun.

Loud staccato bursts came from the front. The ducks took to flight. The wheeled gun was firing at an incredibly rapid rate, each round giving out a deep report that reverberated in my chest. The other SS guards opened up with machine pistols. Those who made a run for it were mowed down instantly. I went for the ground. Most of us, I believe, had accepted their fates and either stood or lay on the ground until the bullets struck.

Moritz lay to my left. He gave me a look of fond farewell and turned to the ground, closing his eyes. His head jolted back violently as a bullet struck his temple. A man fell on top of me as rounds struck him. Another body fell on me from my right. The massacre continued. I heard men scream and cry. I heard thumps as bullets struck and bodies fell.

The guns fell silent. I heard the indistinct voices of SS guards, then metallic sounds. They were reloading the gun. The fusillade erupted once more. I heard more thumps as bullets struck people and corpses. I felt jolts as bullets struck bodies on top of me. In a macabre way, I was protected.

The shooting stopped again. SS guards walked down the hill and stepped through the piles of bodies, occasionally finding someone alive or at least twitching, then finishing him off. One guard stepped on my hand with his thick boot.

"We're done here. Back to camp." I squinted and saw the SS wheel that immense gun around and head for Dachau. One looked back briefly at the carnage then he too made for camp.

I lay there for at least an hour, afraid to move. Blood ran down on me from the corpses but I still didn't move. Behind me I heard the ducks once again, paddling in the stream, searching for food.

This is your signal to get up, Herman, I said to myself. *You have to find the strength to stand up and get away from here.*

I was paralyzed with fear.

You have to get up, Herman – now!

I moved a hand to the front and came upon a motionless torso. A simple effort normally, it expended a considerable amount of my limited energy. I pushed one leg back then the other, and used the leverage to slowly raise up. There in the bright late morning light were dozens of corpses, grotesquely arrayed along the grassy river bank, blood splattered on the striped uniforms and reeds.

My pant leg felt heavy and wet. I reached down and felt a sticky fluid – blood. I panicked as I thought I'd been shot but then realized I was in no pain. Someone else's blood had soaked into my clothing. So many dead.

I have to get out of here.

I heard a muffled groan near me and saw an unsteady hand move. It was Moritz! A bullet had made a dreadful wound on his head, but he was alive all the same. He tentatively felt the blood and the edges of the wound and murmured, "I was shot in the head . . . I was shot in the head."

I looked closely at the wound and saw jagged pieces of skull and splotches of bloody hair. I knew of no words for that situation. None.

"I am dead . . . I was shot in the head, and I am dead."

"No, you're not dead, Moritz." I clasped a hand on his shoulder.

"I am dead . . . I was shot in the head, and I am dead."

"Look at me, Moritz, look at me! There are many dead people here and you are certainly not one of them."

I helped him up but he immediately crumpled to his knees.

"I am not going to make it."

"Yes, you are. Stand up. Stand up. Many people get shot in the head and survive."

I don't know where my expertise in head wounds came from that morning, but my words had their intended effect. He stood up and looked at me.

"Slight pain . . . but not too bad. There are worse things."

"See? The wound isn't serious."

"Yes . . . yes. I think you're right. I feel good enough. Let's get away from here."

So, a boy and a man with bullet hole in his head walked away from the slaughter and knelt at the edge of the stream to clean our hands and clothing. We heard motion behind us and saw a few others rising from the dead and stumbling for the water. Soon there was about five of us, ranging from youths to a man in his fifties.

"Murderers," said one. "This was cold blooded murder."

Again I looked back at the pile of dead – the most recent case I'd seen of the Third Reich's barbarity. I felt that by surveying the scene, taking it in, I was showing courage and paying respect, not just fleeing in horror.

After a few solemn moments I suggested that we head into the woods. After all, the SS might come by, perhaps with another group chosen to cut wood along the river beneath the hill.

Into the forest we went.

We came to an opening and could see rows of plants and animal pens, though not a single person. I entered a barn hoping to find something to eat. The door creaked eerily as it swung open and I saw two men and a woman. Local farmers, I judged. The men were balling hay and the woman was brushing a horse. They stared at us, and we at them. It was clear who we were. They would help us, I thought, just as Emil the Polish farmer had helped me.

"Jews!" one of the men exclaimed angrily, pointing a finger at us then grabbing a pitchfork.

Rather than compliment the fellow on his keen observation, I ran back toward the woods with the others. They chased us with pitchforks and shovels but relented once we were well into the woods.

We ate berries and rested. Where were we? Which way was Dachau? Were German soldiers nearby? There was no way of knowing.

Moritz's wound was sickening to look at. His thin hair was matted over the wound. A trail of black, hardened blood had formed down his face and neck. But he devoured berries and seemed alert.

I mentioned my previous forays into the woods and said that it was best to stay in hiding. When one young man said we should look for partisans, I told him to forget those stories. We got up and walked through the forest, looking for more food and a creek.

We came upon a dirt road. I heard the roar of motor vehicles in the distance. They were getting closer. I motioned for the others to get back into the woods, but I stayed at the edge, watching. They were military vehicles and coming toward us, making clangs and screeches.

They were tanks. But whose?

"They're German," someone said from the woods amid the noise.

I didn't think they were German. I'd seen panzers on railroad tracks and on convoys, but these were shaped differently – higher off the ground. A few foot soldiers were ahead of the column and on either side of it.

"Russians?" someone offered in tentative voice.

I shook my head. "They're coming from the west. The Russians would be from the east."

Three of our band retreated into the forest but Moritz and I stayed put. The tanks grew nearer. *What if they turn out to be Germans,* I asked myself. I offered myself no reply. I walked onto the dirt road and awaited to learn whose army was advancing on me.

The lead tank lurched to a noisy stop fifty meters in front of us, its mighty engine idling loudly. Two foot soldiers warily approached us. They lowered their rifles as they saw two filthy, emaciated, bloodstained apparitions. The commander of the lead tank hopped down and came to us. The three stared at us and conferred briefly. Then one of them said, "Hello, boys . . . we are Amerikaner. Versteh? Amerikaner . . . GIs."

I was elated, overjoyed, and bewildered by the sudden lifting of death from over me. The others came out of the forest and cheered the GIs.

I'd lived through it. Incredibly, I'd lived through it.

LIBERATION

W E SAT DOWN ALONG THE road and wept. Days ago we were slaves. Hours ago we were mowed down along a stream. Now we were free. Free men, free boys.

More American soldiers climbed down from their tanks and half-tracks and looked upon the collection of stickmen and scarecrows in strange garb. Some of us hugged our liberators and sang religious songs to them. We picked up one GI and held him high above our shoulders. A medic saw to Moritz and that was the last I saw of him.

The Americans gave us water and C-rations and even chocolate bars. They were horrified by the sight of us and couldn't understand what had happened to us. Many were angry. We told a German speaker of the camps and of the one nearby – Dachau. An officer asked us to lead them there but most wanted no part it. I agreed to show them the way and in a few moments a young Hungarian boy sat atop a mighty Sherman tank, clanging its way down a Bavarian road at the head of a column of armored vehicles and infantry. No rifle butt or bullet could harm me, or so it felt. It was impossible not to feel powerful and proud and even victorious. And it was impossible not to think that vengeance was at hand. I'd seen it on more than one face.

I navigated the best I could from recalling my march from the river bank and with the help of army maps, we were soon a few hundred meters from the gates of Dachau. There were no guards leading columns of inmates off to work. The camp was motionless.

The watchtowers were still manned. I wanted the Americans shoot them but I was hardly in command. Above the din of tank engines I heard inmates shouting, then there was gunfire.

"They're shooting prisoners," the tank commander said.

Immediately the Americans fired short machine-gun bursts into the watchtowers, sending bright tracer streaks across the sky. Chunks of concrete flew off the towers. Hands went up, guards scurried down.

The GIs warily entered the camp and were greeted by hundreds of jubilant inmates streaming out of the blocks and lining up along the fences shouting, "Americans! Americans!" The newly freed men cried, laughed, and hugged the GIs, then cried more. The Americans were dumbfounded by thousands more stickmen and scarecrows.

I warned that there were worse things to come. "Many dead . . . you must know . . . many, many dead."

Patrols went out across the camp and occasional firefights were heard, usually short ones. The yanks found piles of rotting corpses. It was remarkable, and in a way gratifying, to see their reactions to something that had become a daily routine to me. They'd undoubtedly seen much as they fought their way across France and Germany, but nothing had prepared them for this. Many covered their faces to keep out the terrible stench as much as possible.

An American and I entered several blocks and found people lying in their bunks, unable to believe that the ordeal was over and that they were free. Some were in advanced states of malnutrition and despair, and I wondered if they'd be able to survive even the next few hours.

In an open area between blocks, a few GIs were beating an SS guard. One GI was shouting angrily at the cowering, semi-conscious guard. Maybe the GIs had caught him redhanded in some horrible act, maybe it was simply rough justice. Another GI poured gasoline on him and handed me a box of matches.

There was no hesitation. I thought of countless acts of cruelty I'd seen inflicted on friends and relatives – in selections, on worksites, and in gas chambers – and determined that this young SS guard would pay for them. He looked at me fearfully though in resignation as I lit a match and tossed it on him. He shrieked wildly until a GI put a bullet through his head. I watched the corpse burn in bright yellow and orange flames, sending dark smoke skyward.

I felt neither remorse nor relief, but I wanted no more vengeance. Judging by the sounds across the camp, reprisals went on for quite some time. The dark, unreasoning spirit of revenge was everywhere. GIs handed prisoners rifles and many SS guards were shot or bludgeoned to death. I heard single shots and also long machine-gun bursts. Some shots were preceded by desperate pleas.

So strange to roam about freely and to feel comfortable and even safe around soldiers. There were new discoveries. The GIs found mass graves and cattle cars filled with corpses. The SS had tried to take prisoners elsewhere but fled, leaving the men inside to die and rot. The Death Express had been halted, though.

Hours later, American news people, both men and women, arrived and were also sickened. A jeep with a minister came into the camp and after looking about, he gathered inmates and soldiers around him for a prayer service. I did not join in.

I later learned it was April 29, 1945.

After a day of celebration and retribution, liberators and liberated began to systematically care for survivors. There were many who died within a day or two of liberation. I'm grateful that they at least died free men.

The blocks were increasingly empty. I entered one that was completely empty and thought of the despair that had been in me for so long. Boys my age had schooling and hopes and plans. They played with friends and yearned to kiss pretty girls. My heart was devoid of those things. Friends and girls I'd known and cared for were dead.

I remained in Dachau for several days, eating GI chow and getting stronger. Where would I go? There were many of us who of course despised the camps but felt strangely safe there now. Outside, the Reich was in its death throes, and still dangerous. Inside, paradoxically, I was safe.

My aunt and uncle were dead. My cousin Yanosh? I had no idea where he might be. There was no telling what Hungary and Romania were like in the spring of 1945, however I knew I would try for those places once the Reich was completely defeated.

More and more medics, nurses, and doctors arrived. The foot soldiers and tankers had gone on. I hoped they'd live through what was left of the war and go home to their families.

The army brought in field mess units to prepare meals. There was an immense oven that baked bread for thousands of us. One mess sergeant broke eggs inside GI helmets and made scrambled eggs. Yankee ingenuity, I believe it's called. He warned us not to eat too much or we'd damage our insides. Most of us knew that, or soon learned. Some of us knew but ate voraciously anyway.

News people were everywhere taking pictures and interviewing former prisoners. Benjamin would have been the first to give witness. I made no effort to go to them. One reporter, however, saw me looking on and approached me. He asked, in German, if he could ask me questions. I consented, less reluctantly than I thought when I first saw him.

"What can you tell Americans about Dachau? How long were you here?"

I didn't know where to begin. Oradea? Auschwitz? A Polish farm? What did this neatly attired man want to know? Could I explain what had happened over the last few months? I began to talk and went on for a long time. I don't know how much I said, how much I left out, what the chronology was, or if it made any sense. How could a fifteen-year-old explain the last year? I do recall that he was aghast.

"You're a brave young man, Herman. It's amazing you've lived through this."

I nodded, probably rather blankly.

"Last question. Do you feel that you were just lucky to have survived all this or do you think there was someone looking over you and protecting you?"

I tried to make sense of his words.

"You mean like the Lord or something like that?"

"Yes."

He looked at me, expecting words of moving piety and strong faith for his article to uplift his readers in America.

"After all I've seen with my eyes, I cannot believe there is a greater power looking over me or anyone else in the world."

I motioned to the blocks and stickmen and remaining corpses of Dachau, and I knew there were other places across Germany and Poland and elsewhere too in all likelihood.

The reporter was taken aback. It was probably something he'd only expect from an embittered older person upon whom life had not smiled and upon whom disappointments and failures had accumulated. But there in front of him was a boy of fifteen.

"Another last question then. Do you hate the German people?"

I thought about his question for a while and looked deep inside myself. Do I? Do I hate the Germans? I thought of the death march from Gross-Rosen and the German villagers who looked on in horror and wanted to help.

"No, I don't. The Germans didn't do this. It's individual. Every person acted individually in this war. There were murderers. Many, many of them killed innocent people and did so eagerly. But I'm sure there are good Germans, good Austrians. I know there are good Poles."

"Remarkable. Thank —"

"But I do hate Nazis." I added abruptly. I felt my face turn into an angry scowl.

He looked at me for a while. I think he tried to imagine himself inside Dachau or places like it. I knew he couldn't and if he thought he could, he was wrong. I thought him lucky for not knowing, but decent for trying. We shook hands and went in different directions.

Looking back on that conversation I know the spirit of religion and the faith in a benign deity had perished inside me, replaced by an abiding disdain for supposedly uplifting creeds. Religion was a system of lies, perhaps well intended and often benign, but lies nonetheless. They were akin to what was told to people on the selection platform, or on the way across the tracks, or as they were marched to the river bank to chop wood. "Put your clothing on the hook . . . hot soup awaits you . . . implements will be here shortly . . . it's all part of God's plan."

Life is cruel and violent. People should recognize it as such, and not hide behind lies and false hopes and faith in an uncaring sky.

A FREE MAN

I WALKED OUT THROUGH THE GATES of Dachau and read the inscription above the gate – Arbeit Macht Frei, or Work Makes You Free. I had no idea that the words would become so infamous and sickly paradoxical, but there they were. I had certainly worked and, thanks to the American army, I was free. But where would I go? What would I do?

How many of us had dreamed of walking out the gates of one camp or another on our own terms? So many of us never saw the day.

I came upon one of the GIs who was on administrative duty, both in the camp and in surrounding villages as well, as I would soon learn. He asked if I had family to go to and I told of my aunt and uncle and my hope for Yanosh. When he asked where I was going, I had no answer. I was just walking away and hoping to find something until the war ended in Hungary and Romania, where I might still have family.

He thought a moment then asked me to follow him. We hopped into an army jeep and headed to a village not far from Dachau.

We pulled over and walked. I kept thinking that at any moment guards would pop up and seize me. In my mind I was still hunted. When I did see German soldiers, they were unarmed and being led by GIs, who were indeed armed. There wasn't any confidence in those German faces. They were beaten and they knew it. Now I knew it.

We came to a row house and he rapped loudly on the door. Two German women, a mother about forty-five and daughter of twenty, peered cautiously from the partially opened door. The GI shoved open the door, strode in unceremoniously, and sternly addressed the women in heavily accented German.

"This is Herman. He was a prisoner at Dachau, a place I trust you know of."

He didn't wait for a nod or anything. They were anxious and I presume they knew of the camp. I didn't feel very comfortable and wanted to leave, but I stayed and learned.

"Herman needs a bath, good food, and decent clothing. He is a friend of the United States Army and today that has great importance in your country, as it will for quite some time. I will leave Herman here with you good burghers. When I return in the morning I expect to find him well bathed, well fed, and well dressed. In short, I expect to find a new young man. *Verstehen sie?*"

I looked at the GI rather quizzically.

"Look, Herman, these people knew about the camp and didn't do a goddam thing. Well, now they will make partial amends." And with that, he glared at the women and bade us farewell. As he exited the doorway, he turned to me with a smile. "By the way, young man, you stink!"

I felt very awkward there with strangers, albeit defeated, intimidated ones. I said I would just leave but they insisted I stay, partly out of guilt, partly out of good manners, but mostly out of concern with disappointing the emissary of the United States Army.

They looked at my thin frame and asked, "Didn't they feed you anything?"

It was a question better suited for a different time and place. Then it dawned on them, hard. They'd heard rumors, now they saw evidence.

Well, they drew a bath for me and handed me clean, middle-class attire that once belonged to the mother's son. They didn't mention where he was but I suspected he was of military age. My first bath since . . . since when? Oradea? It was a pleasure, a luxury. A wonderful feeling drew me into a pleasing distant past. The soap was slightly perfumed, and in time so was I. The clothing was too large on me but I felt great. Civilization was returning to me.

They prepared a decent meal that evening. Clearly, however, the American soldiers had more food than these Germans did. Still, they put on a good table and I sat there with a fork, knife, and spoon. Oh, and a cloth napkin.

Without any prompting from me, they spoke of the day the Jews of the village were taken away. They said they regretted it, but I wasn't sure at what point they came to regret it. I wondered how much they knew and how much they diligently avoided knowing, dismissing it as rumor, hearsay, idle talk amid war. I told them what fate likely befell the Jews of their village – cattle cars and forced labor and gas chambers. They did not dismiss it as exaggeration, nor did they nod politely to conceal skepticism. As human beings they were aghast, as Germans they were ashamed

"Oh God," the mother murmured. "I am sure that very bad days are coming for Germany. They're already here. People around the world will hate us for generations to come. I cannot blame them, I cannot blame them. I would hate us too." The daughter was silent but clearly distraught. Her face was drawn and fretful.

Over the years it has become commonplace to greet German claims of ignorance with skepticism if not dismissal. And while I can speak only of two women, I believe they knew bad things went on not far from their dwelling. They knew worse things went on in Poland. They were spared the details and made no great effort to learn them.

Defeat forced them to realize that the Reich's boasts of superior civilization and invincible armies were lies. Defeat also made them receptive to what I said of the Reich and to what they would hear in months and years to come, especially at Nuremberg.

The meal and conversation ended, and I went to the room they prepared for me. In a few moments, I was asleep. A few hours later I had to get up suddenly and race for the outhouse. Too much food. When I returned my bedding was alive with lice and fleas. They'd come from me, even after the bath. Civilization was returning to me, just not as smoothly as I hoped.

A few hours later came the first rays of the sun and I decided to leave. I left a note thanking them then slipped out the door. Once again, I was on my way to some place or another.

The town was in chaos. Former inmates roamed the streets. One told me that Hitler was dead and Germany surrendered the previous day. Welcome news indeed. Some of them broke into abandoned stores and homes and took what they wanted. I came across some *Reichsmarks* and took enough to last me a while.

One group invited me to join them as they broke into a watch store. My new clothing didn't hide my status as a former prisoner. I was still one of them. I thought it best not to be judged a German boy at that particular time. I stood on the street and thought the store was a fine establishment in its day, though not this day. The former inmates broke into vitrines and closets and took whatever they could carry. I went in a moment after the others left and found a few watches and more *Reichsmarks*.

I happened upon a train station where there was great chaos. I thought there was trouble. But it was simply people going about their business without being in rows and columns. GIs and German civilians were all about. Normalcy was returning. I was able to exchange the *Reichsmarks* for scrip and coins.

I bought a ticket for Munich. It was the only place on the board I'd heard of and the map indicated it was a rail hub. From Munich I boarded a train for Prague and after a few stations, we came to an area controlled by the Red army. Russian soldiers came into the cars and demanded our watches. I surrendered two of my prized but short-lived possessions. There was something celebratory about the process. Amid the euphoria of the war being over, it didn't seem so much armed robbery as rewarding the victors.

Watchless and alone, I laughed extensively. I was free and a new life lay before me somewhere. I'd get another watch someday.

Prague was a peaceful city on a gently flowing river. I bought a loaf of bread from a bakery that was obviously struggling to get by. A skinny boy with money was most welcome. I stood on a bridge and heard the occasional sounds of people still celebrating the end of the Second World War. Looking out on the city lights of Prague reminded me of doing the same in Oradea from a ghetto rooftop.

A girl, no more than twelve, approached me and asked if I was a soldier. I replied that I was not. As she neared I could tell she hadn't bathed in a while. Hunger was on her face.

"My name is Ina."

"I'm Herman."

"Do you have anything to eat or some money you can spare?"

I tore off a piece of bread and watched her devour it. I gave her more.

"Thank you. I am sorry – I don't usually ask from strangers but I was so hungry."

I nodded and tore off still more. She ate quietly and upon ingesting the last morsel, her curiosity awakened.

"Where are you from? I can hear an accent."

"It's a long story. I arrived today from Munich."

"What did you do there?"

"I was in a nearby prison camp called Dachau."

The name meant nothing to her.

"My parents died during the war and I've been alone since. I used to work in a grocery store but it had to close, and I haven't had a job for weeks. I haven't eaten for so long, until now. I'm sure it shows."

Something dawned on her.

"Are you a Jew?"

I nodded and for a moment felt discomfort.

"So am I. My parents died in Terezin."

I'd heard of the place from others. It was also called Theresienstadt.

"And Dachau was another camp?" she asked.

I nodded once more and said it was a topic for another time – words that served me well for decades.

Ina offered to show me some of her city and I suggested we both might first find a place to bathe. She smiled, without any embarrassment, and escorted me to a public facility.

We spent a few days together. The money was holding out. There were gardens and parks and monuments. It was a welcome re-acquaintance with peace and life. But I wanted to get back to Hungary and Romania to find out what I could about my family.

I told Ina and she looked downward and murmured, "I wouldn't mind going to Hungary with you."

She wouldn't mind going to Hungary with me. Ah, what clever ways females have!

"Yes, I don't have anyone here anymore."

Sad eyes are another of their ways.

Well, she was a helpless waif in the aftermath of another of Europe's bloodlettings, as was I. So right after breakfast two waifs set out by train for Oradea.

ORADEA AND FOCSANI

A FTER THE DEATHS OF SO many friends and relatives, and after so much upheaval and so many separations, it was important to reconnect with someone. Ina suited admirably.

We took a train to Vienna then another to Oradea, which was in the process of reverting to Romanian rule. It took two days as so many tracks and stations and switching stations had been damaged. Bombers and retreating armies aren't the gentlest things.

I was pleasantly surprised on arriving at Oradea. I expected to see bombed out blocks, piles of rubble, and hopeless faces. However, the city had been fortunate. Damage was slight and limited to a few districts. Shops were open, people went about their day, though with Russian soldiers here and there.

We headed to my neighborhood, partially retracing the path I took when we were marched to the ghetto and later to the cattle cars. I didn't mention any of that to my companion. It was a day of wonder and discovery.

The house of my uncle and aunt looked little changed. I almost expected to see school friends coming down the street for a visit. My mind reeled. I knocked on the door and in time a man in his fifties answered and looked at us cautiously. I told him that I used to live in the house and he looked at me with indifference.

"I bought this place from the city a year ago."

He must have wondered why I was there. At that moment, I wondered the same thing. I had no claim on the place. If anyone did, it was my aunt and uncle, both dead, or Yanosh, whose fate I didn't know. A war and a Final Solution had taken place in the last year. History had passed through my former neighborhood without me.

"My aunt and uncle lived in this house. I grew up here."

"Mine now. I got the place cheap – fully furnished too."

Something came to him.

"Are you Jewish?"

I nodded.

"I see. We heard things. Terrible, terrible things. Wait a moment."

He went inside for a moment and returned with a few items which he handed to me, surprisingly gently I thought. There were several cracked and faded pictures of Joseph, Catalina, and Yanosh. I came upon one with a young boy. "Aha, that's me – the little one in the picture. And that's my aunt holding me. I'm in my school clothes!"

As I showed the pictures to Ina, he went for another thing. "This was here too."

It was a silver cup. Our Kiddush cup.

"I was hoping that someone would pick these up one day. Didn't want to throw them away. Memories – for someone. Good luck to you both."

The door closed, not rudely by any means, though there was a decided finality to it.

We walked around Oradea. I showed Ina my school, the parks I played in, and the government building where I encountered the German soldiers bearing chocolate gifts. My memories were of a city and way of life that was gone. How many of the people I knew only a year earlier were now dead – from the camps, the war, and whatever else those months had served up?

Oradea held nothing, however I wanted to see one more place – the Oradea Mare ghetto. Ina wanted no part of it but I insisted and promised the visit would be brief.

It was a cold unpleasant hour. It was there that I was shown intimations of what would later become known as the Holocaust. The streets were empty, as they were in the last days of the liquidation, as they were when our time came. I showed Ina the house we lived in and the hospital I worked in.

I pointed to the Dreher, where the gendarmes tortured people in an effort to get them to confess the locations of hidden valuables. I stared at it for several moments, imagining blows hitting home and cries of pain, but hearing only rattling windows and creaking doors as winds swept down the debris-strewn street. The Dreher was once again an abandoned brewery.

"Let's go," I said. "There's nothing here anymore."

On to Focsani.

I found the way to the Rittman place, more easily than expected. I'd visited it a few times, but not in many years. I rapped on the door, half expecting another gruff stranger with a handful of old mementoes.

A young man answered. He studied me for a while then tentatively asked, "Are you Shuly? It's me – your brother Motzu!"

"I knew it," I exclaimed. I didn't recognize him at all, actually.

Two long-separated brothers embraced. I introduced Ina and in we went. The small rooms and sparse furniture looked familiar yet alien, as though from a play I'd seen long ago. So much had transpired since I'd been there last. I felt at once both son and visitor.

Two young women looked at me then shouted, "Oh my, oh my!" It was my sisters Rosy and Viorica.

My mother came to see what the commotion was about.

"Oh my! It can't be, it can't be! Is that you? Is that really you, Shuly?" She wept, her hands trembled.

"Yes, it's your Shuly, mother!"

I ran to her arms.

"We heard such terrible things about what happened in Hungary! We tried to get word from Oradea but there was none to be had. I thought I'd never see my littlest one again. Where were you? Why are you so skinny?"

A river of questions followed, most which I managed to elide. I introduced Ina once again and added that we wouldn't mind a bite to eat. A light meal was immediately served up.

As we ate, my mother inquired again why I was so thin. She asked as though I simply hadn't been eating well while away at boarding school. Then she gasped, "Shuly, were you in a Nazi camp?"

I nodded reluctantly.

"Oh my, oh my! What about Joseph and Catalina?"

My saddened face answered the question but I felt obliged to come out and say they'd been killed. Mother and the others wept. I added that I'd seen Yanosh last year and hoped he might have come through it, but that his wife and children had shared Aunt Catalina's fate.

My father, Shlomo, raced home from his restaurant on receiving word of my arrival, and toward the evening we all had dinner. The reunion was pleasant. My family was never so strong and warm as it was that night. Nonetheless, I didn't feel entirely part of it.

My brothers, I learned, had been recently released from Romanian work camps. The labor was harsh, but they looked well. Jews were more fortunate in Romania. The Third Reich's reach was less than it was into Hungary and elsewhere. Focsani was especially fortunate. I marveled that my aunt and uncle's home was only a few kilometers from the Romanian border then. Yet the short distance made an immense difference to those on the Hungarian side of the line.

They looked at me expectingly, as though I should recount experiences of my travels across Europe. Looking at the genteel surroundings, I said that there were many stories to tell, mostly of an unpleasant nature, and that this was not the time to go over them. A thousand memories passed through me – events that would sicken them and haunt them. I closed the door on the past.

I settled into family life more easily than we thought possible on those evenings outside the blocks before lights out, but my past had not been shared by family members. It had no connection with anyone else in my family. I was pleased to see Ina feel at home.

She and I played soccer in the park. Quite the young athlete, she was. A tomboy, one might say. Two children had been tossed about by Europe's worst storm, and had now found a safe haven.

I found odd jobs around Focsani and tried to pitch in with the household. Opportunities weren't bountiful in those days.

My brother Lucian announced one day that he felt confined and wanted to move elsewhere. Many of his friends talked of emigrating to America. The idea appealed to Motzu as well. America was a land of wealth and opportunity, Romania was one of poverty and stagnation – and Russian occupation. My parents objected sternly. The family was back together after many years, and it was going to stay that way. Parents commanded respect back then. Their statements were law, not suggestion.

The idea of moving on stayed with me. Perhaps it was because my principal family was dead, perhaps because I'd done so much moving about in the last year, perhaps because I could never feel at home anywhere anymore.

My brothers held fast to the idea of emigrating until they simply determined to go. Motzu decided to leave for Budapest and from there, for America. Lucian would stay at home for now but would soon follow.

I wanted to go too, and discussed it with Ina. When I told her she was welcome to stay in Focsani with my family, she was offended, even hurt. I was her family. She insisted on being with me and I could not say no to someone who had come to rely on me.

Motzu, Ina, and I set out on our way to Budapest where we'd heard there were businesses that arranged emigration to America. The city was in flux. People coming home after the war, people moving on to other places, former soldiers wandering about. Nothing was permanent anymore.

New people came and went and with them were new ideas, among them Zionism. There was a new country to be built by energetic young people – Israel. The word then denoted only an ancient past and a place where a handful of idealists had gone over the last few decades to scratch out hard lives.

The leaders of a Zionist group in Budapest told us of the ancient land and our people's role in it, from Moses to the Diaspora to visionaries like Theodor Herzl. More practically, they told us of the warm climate, open spaces, freedom, and oranges. Oranges had a magical attraction to me. Ina and I listened and expressed our interest. Motzu was unimpressed by the talks, but he gave in after a few more evenings.

We went through a training course in Budapest where there were scores of young curious people like us. Excitement was everywhere. New friendships were made for the new land. Motzu met a young woman there, Ilana, and was smitten. A few weeks later they married.[10]

One instructor, Haim Yanai, had been sent from Israel to give longer and more in-depth lectures and to encourage us to make the decision to emigrate – or "Make Aliyah." Most of the world called it Mandate Palestine, he always called it Israel.

We were given pen and paper and we took notes on the history of the Jewish people and their ancient land on the eastern Mediterranean. The lectures covered everything from the time of Abraham to the present. We also learned, there in the middle of Budapest, how to live on a farm with little in the way of tractors or implements. The whole process took about six months and I look back upon it as absolutely wonderful. A new day was dawning and we would be part of it.

---

[10] They remain so to this day and in fact celebrated seventy years of marriage not long ago.

ALIYAH BEGINS

YANAI GATHERED US IN THE dining room where a light meal was spread out on serving tables. He was a handsome, charismatic, athletic fellow who dressed in simple attire, and when he spoke we listened intently, some raptly. It was October of 1946 and the hum of the heaters could be heard above the sounds of diners and the speaker.

He explained that the British didn't allow any more European Jews to settle in Mandate Palestine. Their navy kept our ships from entering port and their soldiers patrolled the borders. Many of our ships nonetheless tried to get through. Some made it. The passengers were met by underground settlement networks and began new lives on farms or kibbutzes. Other ships were seized. The passengers were placed in refugee camps on Cyprus or, temporarily, in the Mandate.

Yanai scanned the assembly proudly, as though a patriarch before his progeny.

"You're ready! You've been taught about our country – its past, present, and future. Now it is time to take the step. Our people are waiting for you there. They will help you start a new life. It will not be easy. Not at all. You'll dig and plant seeds, you'll toil in cramped factories, you'll guard perimeters, and you'll even work in dining rooms, preparing food and washing dishes. But the rewards are limitless. It will be *your* country – a country no one will be able to take from you. No one can humiliate you or make you suffer ever again. You can raise your families freely and with dignity. You will play important roles in *creating* the new country."

I looked around and saw a sea of bright, eager faces. Most of them were enthralled by Yanai, especially the women. I liked what he was saying, and I indeed wanted to go to the new land, but I must say his oratory, and the crowd's breathless acceptance of his every word, amused me.

"In a week we shall travel to a city named Bakar. It is near Rijeka, in Yugoslavia. As we've learned, British ships patrol the seas around Israel. They seek to interdict our vessels and prevent us from reaching their land. We have a plan to get around them."

The room fell silent save for the loud heaters. We would be part of this plan. Our success in reaching the new land depended on it.

"Two ships will be leaving Bakar. A large one named *The Jewish Resistance Movement*[11] and a smaller one named *Anastasia*, or as it's called, "the Saint." The plan is to deceive the British ships. The Saint will transfer her people to the larger ship near Greece and then attract the British navy's attention. The British will catch her and her crew, and return them to Europe. The British will be pleased with their catch, and you will be on your way to safety on the shores of Israel!"

The room became loud with murmurs, questions, and comments. Most felt they were in good hands. Many, however, found the plan rather unconvincing and filled with risk. Motzu and Ilana, Ina and I, did. It was too simple, as though the British were overworked school monitors and we were clever students.

Yanai held out his arms to quiet the room and spoke loudly.

---

[11] The ship was also named העברי המרי תנועת – later changed to *Knesset Israel*.

"It will not be easy. It will not be easy. The larger ship will not have enough room for all of you to travel in comfort. The conditions will be unpleasant but it will be for only a few days. You have to be strong. And remember – this all we have and we *have to* succeed. We have to reach the land of Israel, at any cost."

He spoke with greater strength and determination than before. Charm gave way to will. That was Yanai, that was his organization. They were determined to bring us to Israel and create the new nation, at any cost.

On November 5, 1946 four thousands of us gathered in the port of Bakar. The atmosphere was optimistic and joyful. The Yugoslavian government was helpful. Having been occupied by the Third Reich, and having suffered immense casualties fighting it, Yugoslavia was willing to help those who'd also suffered at German hands.

The Prime Minister, Josip Broz, better known as Tito, visited the port to see how preparations are going. It was said he directed the fiercest partisan resistance in all Europe. That impressed me. The local people greeted us and every night brought us bread and cakes. They spent time with us and exchanged stories in broken German.

We received a gift from the Tito government. Three hundred German prisoners of war were sent to help prepare our ships. Many people were angered by their presence but Yanai insisted we show them no malice.

"Our greatness is in not stooping to their level. We are humans and we will treat other people as humans, even if their countrymen did terrible things to us in the recent past. If we do them harm, we become like them."

His words were stated forcefully and thoughtfully. We treated the POWs well.

Motzu and Ilana, Ina and I, lived in a hostel rented by the Jewish Agency named "Sochnout" (סוכנות). We spent a restless week there. At night I could look out and see the ship illuminated by the harbor lights. Men, some of them German prisoners, were loading crate after crate. One night, word came from Yanai that we would sail in the morning.

It was our last night in Europe. Tomorrow we'd set out for a new land on a different continent. New language, new customs, new people, new lives. I stared out on the harbor, Ina beside me. All my sixteen years had been in Europe.

Ina was less wistful. She was eager to get away from Europe. We would be in a new land that would be *ours*. We would be safe there and we would *make* the land safe. She was echoing Yanai's words, as were many.

I thought of the British and their policy against immigration. I knew nothing of Balfour or the Mandate or the Arab countries around it. And while no one can predict the future, especially in those chaotic years following World War Two, I knew that nothing came easy in this world, and nothing would come easy for a people trying to build a new country anywhere in it.

The next morning, without anything more than nibbles of bread, we marched to the dock. Motzu and Ilana boarded the larger vessel, Ina and I headed for the smaller one – the Saint.[12]

Three men arrived from Israel – the Saint's owner, Yossi Hamburger-Harel ("Amnon"), the captain, Reuven Hirsh Yatir ("Abraham"), and telegrapher Yoash Zidon ("Maty," later a member of the Knesset). All three had the rugged good looks of Israeli pioneers. Every one of us wanted to look like them one day. Americans had movie stars, we had *Sabras*.

As I climbed aboard the Saint the crew said I was to be the last one. Ina was not allowed to board, despite my insistence that she was family. "You'll meet again in Israel, young man. The ship is already overcrowded. You'll be reunited in Israel." Ina was being led away by

---

[12] We were later told that the ship was to be called *Abba Berditzev*, in honor of a man who served, and died, in the resistance in Czechoslovakia.

a member of the organization who echoed the promise of reunion in Israel. I called out to her with the same hope.

A while later the call came for two people to help load late-arriving crates. Though the call was for volunteers, a man pointed to another fellow and me, and down the gangplank we went to become stevedores for an hour. As we pushed a large crate along toward the freight opening, someone joined us. It was Ina. We stored the crates below and the Saint sailed from port a while later with a young stowaway.

As evening came I asked Ina if she would care to join me in the posh dining room where an excellent meal complete with fine wine would be served. Opting not to don evening wear, we walked arm in arm into the cramped, foul-smelling hall and ate rice, potatoes, and a substance that was rumored to be meat. Afterwards we stood on deck and watched the Saint ply the cold, increasingly choppy seas of the Adriatic.

Ina was seasick. We'd been warned of that before boarding. Undoubtedly, the less than elegant dining room and cuisine figured in her illness. I fared better.

Down below, in our fetid bunk area, Ina had to vomit. She lay down, weak and still nauseous. Someone with a measure of medical knowledge said she needed rest and sufficient water to prevent dehydration.

The weather was not on our side. The Adriatic was getting rough and the ship rolled about rather violently. Though hardly a seafaring man, I looked upon the crew with considerable suspicion.

Still unaffected by the seas, I walked about the ship and noticed a great deal of rust on the old vessel. How many voyages had the Saint made already? How many more did she have ahead? I left those questions for the organization and headed to my bunk for some sleep. In any case, we'd soon be transferred to the larger ship.

A few hours later I was awakened by a loud noise and powerful jolt. People looked at one another fearfully. We thought our voyage would be safe until we reached the coast of Israel and the British navy. Something had gone wrong not far from port.

You don't have to be an old salt to know that if a ship's in trouble, it's better to be on deck than below. Many of us had the same thought. One man said we'd hit a sea mine, another was sure we'd been torpedoed. We were dead in the water and though it was noisy from the commotion and high seas, I was pretty sure the engines had stopped.

"No need to be alarmed! Everything's alright."

The crewman's words were dismissive and far from reassuring. Someone pointed to a rocky island in the distance, which I did find reassuring.

After an hour, word came that the engines had broken down. We were adrift and had hit submerged rocks. However, *Knesset Israel* would arrive soon and we'd transfer to her. The weather worsened and waves crashed over the railings. The ship began to list to one side and we were put to work bailing water with whatever we could find. Nevertheless, we continued to list.

"We're going to sink! We're going to sink!" people cried out.

A crewman insisted the ship was in no danger of going under. *Knesset Israel* would arrive soon and besides, the water wasn't very deep.

I continued on the bailing team, handing a bucket from one fellow passenger to another, up the dank stairwells to the railings. We were given time for a short rest after which we quickly returned to duty. The listing stabilized but we were still leaning to one side rather awkwardly.

A loud metallic sound startled us and the ship lurched to its side even more. Some people jumped into the water and made for the island. The loudspeaker system crackled on and the captain gave the order to abandon ship. I raced below to Ina's cabin but found the way blocked by rising water and fallen steel beams.

I called out to her and she pleaded for my help. A passerby and I tried to move the beam for many frantic minutes but a dozen men couldn't have budged it.

We looked at each other and silently agreed there was nothing more to be done. That was clear. Dreadful, but clear. Ina's voice was weak yet charged with panic.

"Shuly! Shuly! Get me out of here!"

I closed my eyes and summoned all my courage.

"Ina, I can't get you out."

"What?"

"I can't get you out of there, Ina. I just can't. We've tried to reach you but we cannot."

"No! No! Please!"

"I'm so sorry, Ina. So sorry."

I could say no more. There was nothing more to say. Ina was doomed. In time, as the water continued to rise, she silently accepted the situation.

"Shuly. . . . Shuly, I want you to know that I understand."

The only sounds were the rushing water and the clamor above. The Saint was sinking faster, water reached my rib cage. The passerby, though eager to get to the deck, showed great compassion, and stood by us.

"Ina, I don't know what to do."

"Shuly, listen. You have to leave now." She was strangely calm. You have to go. Otherwise, you'll die needlessly. The water is rising fast. Please go, Shuly, I don't want you to die."

I closed my eyes and suggested the man head up to the deck, but he still would not leave.

"Shuly?" Ina's voice trembled. "Can you stay a few more minutes? I don't want to die alone."

"I am here, sweet one. I am here."

"I want you to know that you were my family, Shuly. I love you and your family. You were my family. You and they were my family."

"We love you too, Ina, and we always will. I am holding you now. I am with you."

"Oh, the water! I don't want to die! I don't want to die! Oh! Oh!"

I could only hear Ina's small hands pounding on the door. After a few minutes, mercifully, the pounding stopped.

"We have to go, we have to go, now."

The man pulled me toward the stairwell then up to the deck.

We leaped into the choppy water and swam to the rocky island. In the morning the other survivors and I were picked up by lifeboats and taken to *Knesset Israel.* I was given a place to lie down and I fell asleep, as sad and sickened as ever in my life. Another orphan had been lost in a storm.

The morning, at least, brought welcome news. I found my brother Motzu and Ilana. Or rather they found me. There were three of us now.

The captain and crew of *Knesset Israel* imposed a strict regimen on the passengers as we idled in Greek waters for several days. Work forced me out of another bout of despair. I was assigned to a team and we did various chores, especially swabbing out the bunk areas where many people had been seasick. As might be imagined, work on the deck was a welcome break.

At breakfast I heard someone speak my name. "Shuly? Shuly, is that you?"

It was a young man about thirty. He had the look of someone struggling back from emaciation that I'd come to recognize over the last few months. He was one of us. It took a moment or two, then I recognized him. It was Yanosh. Joseph and Catalina's son had survived. I hadn't seen him since a selection in Birkenau sent him to Monovitz. Fortune had placed us on the same ship and we were bound for Israel.

In time, my brother came by and we held an informal reunion – a common enough sight in the postwar years, and a powerfully moving one as well. I learned, to my sorrow, that Yanosh was now sure he'd lost his wife and small children in a Birkenau gas chamber. What strength he and others had.

That evening we spoke more on the deck. We had caught up on our pasts; it was time to talk of our future. Europe was old and dying, much of it lay in ruins. Motzu spoke of the warm weather, farmlands, and oranges of Israel. The land held great promise.

Yanosh saw Israel as an intermediary goal. He wanted to see the new land but then go on to America. Ilana, however, was determined to build a new life in Israel, and that was that. Israel sounded good to me too.

On November 21 we met as scheduled with a fishing boat near Piraeus which took the Greek crew and our skipper, who was slated to head back to Yugoslavia to organize more ships. Our new skipper was Reuben Yatir, his first officer was Yossi Harel. They announced the new plan to hug the shorelines of Cyprus and Lebanon in order to evade the British navy, before steaming south for Israel.

Not long thereafter, a small plane circled us. The captain spread the word that it was a British reconnaissance aircraft and that it had radioed for our identity and destination. We identified ourselves as *Santa Maria* destined for Alexandria, Egypt. Later that day, a British warship came up behind us. His majesty's navy was on to us.

The warship suggested we seek port on Cyprus where we would receive provisions and medical help, if needed. Our captain, I later learned, had an SOP which the *Haganah* had come up with. We clambered below deck as the crew hoisted the Panamanian flag, a common enough sight on merchant ships in the Mediterranean. It fooled no one.

That night Yossi Harel gathered us.

"We have to prepare for the British." He spoke in an assured manner. "Let's not delude ourselves, we will have to confront them but we have to do it in the right way. When we reach Haifa, we will resist them. We will not shoot or even injure any British serviceman. If you have a firearm, you must drop it on the floor. Otherwise they will shoot you and many others as well. We are going to resist the British quarantine policy – but not violently. We will use sticks and buckets, but no firearms. We'll use our moral strength to appeal to the world to allow us into our land."

We sailed past Tripoli in northern Lebanon, the British warship still trailing us. Israel was only a hundred fifty kilometers away. As we neared Israeli waters, three more British ships came in sight. They announced they would board us and we prepared to resist. Some of us were directed to stand on deck. I was one of them.

The British sent launches with an inspection team. They said, quite politely, that we were to be sent back to Europe. Our captain countered that an international court had sanctioned our disembarkation on Israel's soil. As he spoke, the British sailors were taking up positions around the ship. Scuffles broke out as they tried to physically remove people from *Knesset Israel*. We outnumbered them, of course, so we hurled them overboard and prevented them from climbing back up the sides.

The British ships fired tear gas canisters and smoke drifted below decks, including where many children were. Among them were a few babies who'd been born since departing Yugoslavia. Our captain would not risk the lives of babies and children; he gave the order to give in.

The poet Nathan Alterman wrote about the tear gas from a young girl's perspective.

כַּאֲשֶׁר הַפְּצָצָה הַשְּׁלִישִׁית בְּמִסְפָּר
פָּלְטָה זֶרֶם עָשָׁן בְּתַחְתִּית הַסְּפִינָה
הַיַּלְדָּה הֶחָוֶרֶת הִפְשִׁילָה צַוָּאר
יַעֵן שָׂמוּ לְפֶתַע מַחֲנָק לִגְרוֹנָהּ

As the third bomb
Released its choking smoke
A pale little girl held her throat
As all her air was lost.

We were taken to Haifa and housed in an immense aircraft hangar. The food was fairly good, I'll say that, and the blankets made sleeping on the concrete floor less uncomfortable. But I was behind a fence again.

We soon boarded a British ship that took us to a refugee camp on Cyprus. Sad that our first visit to Israel was so brief. We were placed in a large camp. Some of us were fortunate to be billeted in shacks rather than in tents. When people complained of harsh conditions, Yanosh and I would look at each other and enjoy a moment of unspoken, liberating humor.

The British allowed our organization in Israel to send in food, a dental team, and even recreational items, including soccer balls. Soccer is a wonderful past time in almost any condition. We formed our own camp government. We were given a taste of life on a kibbutz.

Months past. Several people I knew managed to escape from the camp and with the help of local Jews, make their way to Israel on small vessels. But life on Cyprus was largely uneventful. We had dances where young people socialized and talented people performed. A few untalented people also performed. British and Israeli speakers told of us life in Israel and in time, the British allowed several hundred people a month to go to Israel.

The stay was not uneventful for everyone. Many babies were born in the camp. Many more were conceived there. Motzu and Ilana had a child in the Cyprus camp.

As I watched a group boarding ship for the voyage to Israel, I saw a young woman who looked familiar. She saw me and a look of partial recognition came to her. Distant places and events whirled in my mind and a name came to me.

"Alexa!"

She looked at me for a moment.

"Herman!"

It was Alexa, the nurse at the hospital in the Oradea Mare ghetto, whose father had died with her by his side. Her group was going up the gangplank so there was no time for a reunion.

"Good luck to you in Israel, Alexa. I'll be there soon."

"Good luck to *you* in Israel."

No more words were exchanged. She was on the deck and being led to quarters.

So, Alexa had survived the ghetto, Auschwitz, and whatever other camps she might have been sent to. She had persevered and she had kept the promise to her father. I'm sure we both thought back to that night in the Oradea ghetto as she climbed aboard ship.

She waved to me one last time.

Not long thereafter, after seven months on Cyprus, we were told that we would board a ship in the morning and sail to Israel. My brother's family and I awaited the hour. This was it. We were on our way. What began many months ago in Budapest was about to come to fruition. Motzu remained skeptical. There was always something that would pop up and ruin even well-made plans.

I asked what we'd do when we got there and no one knew in any detail. A new land was there for us and we'd make something of it. I thought of the oranges.

Motzu asked why I was so pensive and I replied I had an obligation.

"I promised someone – I think it was about a year and half ago – that someday I would write down what I saw in the camps."

"Who?"

"More than one person, but most importantly a man named Benjamin. We marched from Auschwitz to Gross-Rosen together. He died in a quarry. It has to be written down someday."

Motzu must have thought it odd that a seventeen-year-old boy would speak of chronicling those days. I certainly did. And while I wanted to put those days aside and live my life, I knew there were so many others that had had no such life. And I determined, there with my brother and his wife and their baby daughter, that someday I would write them down.

And here we are.

KFAR GILADI

THE NEXT DAY WE SAILED and soon docked in Haifa, which is only 160 kilometers from Cyprus. My brother and cousin wanted to stay in Haifa but on Cyprus I'd heard of a kibbutz called Kfar Giladi. We were saddened at the thought of another separation but Motzu reminded us that Israel was not a vast land and we'd never be very far from each other.

Kfar Giladi is in Galilee, in northern Israel. I'd learned of kibbutzes from the lectures in Budapest and on Cyprus, and the idea appealed to me. People worked together for each other. About forty of us assembled in Haifa and were taken by bus through hills and forests until we came to a settlement in the low mountains. A few armed men and women patrolled the perimeter.

We were greeted and assembled in front of a modest administrative building. A lovely young woman named Naomi, attired in khaki shirt and shorts, welcomed us and told us of apple and olive trees, poultry coops, and dairy cows. The names of elders and an outline of the rules followed. The introduction lasted an hour.

When she asked for questions, my hand shot up. I hesitated for a moment as all eyes were on me, but soon found my words. "My name is Herman Rittman and I have a question, please. Do you have orange trees here?"

Naomi smiled, quite pleasantly too.

"Aha, many newcomers have heard such good things about our fruits. Of course, we have orange trees. Lemons and grapefruits abound here as well. Our orange trees are few in number, though. We don't sell them in the marketplaces. They are for the enjoyment of the kibbutz. Shall we see them now?"

We walked a few hundred meters to a hectare, maybe less, of orange trees. We were encouraged to sample the sweet fruits of Kfar Giladi.

I held a large one still on the branch and felt the cool rind. It was true what they'd said back in Budapest. The oranges of Israel are indeed beautiful. But I didn't want to separate it from its home.

"Go ahead. Pick it," Naomi encouraged. "You'll not ruin anything. A fruit is meant to be enjoyed. We toil; then we enjoy. It's the circle of life, for us and for the children. Welcome to Israel. You are one of us now."

I picked the orange and peeled away the rind, revealing bright, juicy segments separated by soft pulp.

I was a member of Kfar Giladi, and I was an Israeli.

AFTERWORD

I STAYED ON AT THE KIBBUTZ in northern Galilee. It was wonderful, family and home, all I could hope for then. On May 14 1948, Israel was declared an independent nation. We received the news with great joy. However, a few hours later soldiers from Egypt, Jordan, Iraq, Syria, and Lebanon invaded Israel from all sides. Men and women formed a militia to defend the kibbutz. I served.

After the war, I remained in the Israel Defense Forces and took part in the Sinai War of 1956. I led a platoon in the Six-Day War of 1967. I was badly wounded in the Yom Kippur War of 1973 and retired from active duty shortly thereafter. I stayed on with the defense ministry in a wide range of civilian positions. Stories for another day, perhaps.

Many immigrants to Israel change their names. I changed my first name from Herman to Zvi. I married in 1955 and had three children. Two of them live in Israel today. Netanya is my home now.

I never forgot my promise to Benjamin. Nor could I forget the hope of many others that events be recounted. I was ever looking for the opportunity to put my story down in writing. Now, seventy-one years after I walked out of Dachau a free man, my first son has helped me do so.

There are many books that recount those days in the Third Reich's camps, but I think as many of them as possible is for the good. There are thousands of different experiences and they should all be written down. They should all be read and they should all be remembered.

In 1985 I returned to Auschwitz. Friends, some of them Holocaust survivors, had gone there over the years, but I always declined. I finally decided to go. My wife and a few friends went with me.

The plane landed in Krakow and I felt the approach of the unknown. It reminded me, at least somewhat, of what I felt as a fourteen-year-old with my aunt, uncle, and Yanosh on my first arrival. Somewhat. We hired a driver to take us the thirty kilometers to Oswiecim, the Polish village whose name was Germanized into the name of the death camp.

There above the gate was the infamous inscription *Arbeit Macht Frei*. Recognition of a familiar sight usually elicits positive thoughts; it's part of how our minds work. But on seeing those words and the buildings and fields behind the gate, I gasped for air and fought off an unexpected wave of panic. I was able to subdue it without others noticing.

How many times had I arrived here? Yes, this was my third time.

I entered the gate and walked into Auschwitz I. Along the way, I passed a million souls marching the other way, toward Birkenau. There were dirty uniforms, emaciated bodies, and terrified and hopeless faces. I saw Aunt Catalina, Yanosh's wife and children, and others whose names I could not recall or never knew. I searched for a fourteen-year-old boy. On and on they marched. On and on. I looked above and saw sunlight and clear blue sky.

The buildings had been well maintained. They cast shadows on neatly trimmed grass. It could be initially mistaken for an old but not unpleasant historical site. Signs and enlarged photographs and articulate young guides told of the place, who had been there, and what went on there. They were instructive. The visitors learned.

All around us were the fences with their arrays of grotesque electrodes and L-shaped posts, where people chose to go out on their own terms. We took down their stiffened bodies after kapos shut off the power.

Over in Birkenau, I found the building where we ate our meager rations before hurrying off to roll call and work assignments. After some time, and after a few wrong turns, I found among a number of trees the block where I lived upon arrival in the spring of 1944. I walked inside, my companions just behind. The old wood had been preserved with varnish. It was a better smell than the one that came to mind on entry. The wood was cool and smooth to my touch. I walked down the row and stumbled briefly. I pointed out one of the bunks to my wife and friends. "This is where I slept."

At the northern part of Birkenau were the gas chambers and *kremas*. Both seemed unchanged. On entering the anteroom of one of the gas chambers, I could see the shoes and clothes of dead people. I breathed in deeply and smelled only cold cement. The *kremas* were strangely quiet, as they'd been unused since 1945.

We walked to where the trains once arrived. The tracks are still there, but the platform is gone, replaced by a walkway and long grassy stretches. That's what my wife and companions saw. I saw cold spotlights, rifles crashing down on helpless people, snarling dogs, and families torn apart forever.

Tired and somber, we headed out, exiting through the railroad track opening with the forbidding tower atop it. Coming in were a group of young visitors, one carrying the flag of Israel.

I've come to Auschwitz three times now. I will never go there again.

In spite of everything, I still believe that people are really good at heart.

– Anne Frank

PHOTOGRAPHS

Herman (Shuly) – One year old in Focsani, Romania

Herman in school uniform, age 11,
with Uncle Joseph and Aunt Catalina in Oradea, 1941

Herman, age 8, with Uncle Joseph in Alba Julia, Romania

Hermina and Solomon Rittman, ca 1910

Front row: siblings Viorica, Rosy, Motzu Hermina Rittman
is holding her baby Herman. Solomon Rittman is to the
right. The other three women are Hermina's sister

Yanosh and Zvi, 1989, Los Angeles

Yanosh, his wife, and Zvi, 1989, Los Angeles

Zvi and his mother Hermina, 1986. She passed away in 1989.

Zvi and the IDF Soccer Team, 1975

Zvi Rittman with grandchildren Bar and Noa, 2014, Netanya

Motzu, Zvi, and Lucian, 1995, Prague

Lucian, Motzu, and Zvi, 2013, Netanya

Zvi with sons Danny and Alon, 2014, Netanya

Merav Rittman with father Zvi, 2015, Haifa

Zvi and grandson Daniel, 2015, Netanya

Printed in the United States
By Bookmasters